THE ART OF THE

QUILT

THE ART OF THE
QUILT

Ruth Marler

COURAGE BOOKS

AN IMPRINT OF
RUNNING PRESS BOOK PUBLISHERS

First published in 2001 by
PRC Publishing Ltd
8–10 Blenheim Court, Brewery Road, London N7 9NY
A member of the Chrysalis Group plc

Published by Courage Books, an imprint of
Running Press Books Publishers
125 South Twenty-second Street
Philadelphia, Pennsylvania 19103-4399

THE INFORMATION BOXES IN THE SECTION "THE QUILTS" IDENTIFY:

Title or name of quilt

* Quiltmaker, if known, where made; date
* Main fabric used
* height and width
* Where from
* Further information on provenance
  Museum accession number Photographer if known

Feathered Touching Stars Quilt

* Quiltmaker unidentified, Ohio; 1846
* Cotton
* height 85½" width 84¾"
* Collection of the American Folk Art Museum, New York
* Gift of Cyril Irwin Nelson
  1989.17.6 Photo by Matt Hoebermann

Acknowledgments

The American Folk Art Museum, whose new building at 45 West 53rd Street opened in 2001, has an unrivaled collection of American quilts.
Most of the historical material in this book came from this source. We'd like to thank Janey Fire for her help.
All uncredited photographs were supplied courtesy of © Collins & Brown.
The front cover photograph shows the Center Star Crazy Throw by Mary Ann Crocker Hinman (1817-1893), New York State; 1880-1890.
Collection of the American Folk Art Museum, New York. Gift of Ruth E Avard. 1993.2.1. Photo by Matt Hoebermann (see page 65).

The photograph on page 2 shows a Log Cabin quilt (see page 112).

Additional text provided by Dr. Duncan Clarke

CONTENTS

INTRODUCTION

The precise beginnings of the American quilt, an object that is seen by some as a symbol of perfect womanly skills and American tradition, are indeterminate. What is certain is that, before the start of the seventeenth century, three distinct types of textile work were known to exist in different parts of the world. Scraps, remnants, and pieces of worn-out garment were used to create items such as bedcovers; fabric was applied for decorative effect; and padded or quilted textiles were used for warmth. It was the merging of these three skills that resulted in this paradigm of Americanness, the quilt.

From early colonial times, the evolution of the quilt has been an innovative living expression of the people involved rather than a mere static artifact. This book seeks to introduce the reader to the world of that expression: to display the stages of development through which this symbol of America has passed, and to celebrate the diverse methods, designs, and influences that have contributed to what we now recognize as a quilt. A glossary is provided to be used in conjunction with the illustrations to gain

an insight into the methods and skills involved in the making of a quilt.

The act of piecing and quilting is not merely, and never has been, a means of producing a practical, useful item. This act also affords the maker a means of creative expression and a legitimate reason for socializing and participating in what could be looked upon as group advice and counseling sessions. Thus quilt making is one of the few crafts where a group of women, of mixed ability and ages, can congregate for mutual relaxation and help.

Textiles have long been considered to be the woman's realm, and for a considerable period of time this has led to such artistic expressions ranking low in the creative hierarchy. However, when discussing the link between femininity and needlework, Roszicka Parker said in *The Subversive Stitch* that, "women . . . managed to make meanings of their own in the very medium intended to inculcate self-effacement." Contrary, then, to popular belief, quilts are not just hearts, flowers, swags, and log cabins. Many quilts throughout the 300-year span of their existence can be identified as being overtly and blatantly political. Themes range from support for particular politicians or causes to expressions of Civil War allegiance to statements about suffrage and temperance.

The colorful world of quilting—a selection of quilts, some pieced and some appliquéd, displayed for sales.
© William A. Bake/CORBIS

Quilt making is one of the few crafts where a group of women, of mixed ability and ages, can congregate for mutual relaxation and help. © CORBIS

The earliest American quilts to survive are from around the end of the first quarter of the eighteenth century. The majority of these early quilts are what would have been known as "show quilts." Never intended to be used on a daily basis, it is due to their elevated status that they have long outlasted their makers. Initially there were three types of quilt—wholecloth, medallion, and mosaic piecework, in which one shape is repeated all over the quilt. What has come to be known as "blockwork" did not, however, come into existence until the early nineteenth century. Frequently, quilts that crossed the three original types were constructed with a central medallion, some large expanses or strips of cloth, interspersed with pieced blocks in basic geometric shapes, repeated many times, with the quilting stitches that attached the top to the other layers providing a final element of decoration.

Wholecloth quilts were made from a large expanse of one fabric, although several pieces might have to be joined together to achieve the dimensions required. It has been argued that in the earliest days of the history of the American quilt, the original width of a piece of fabric was preserved and cherished as cloth was imported, highly priced and, therefore, prized. Many early wholecloth quilts were of one solid color and made of "calimanco," a fine-glazed wool cloth, with the quilting stitches and patterns providing the decorative content. Other wholecloth quilts utilized patterned fabric and, therefore, the quilting was of a more utilitarian nature, serving only to unite the quilt top with the filling and the backing. Any elaborate quilting

patterns would have been hidden by the exotic and oriental prints.

A third type of wholecloth quilt was known as "whitework," where both the top and the backing would have been of white cotton or linen. The discovery of buried classical cities such as Herculaneum and Pompeii gave rise to the style known as Neoclassicism. In the American textile world this celebration of classical purity manifested itself in the production of all-white quilts in which the decorative element was provided by the use of intricate stitching and padding that transformed a flat area of cloth into a low-relief. Techniques such as cording, trapunto, and candlewicking or roving were employed to achieve this effect. Cording and trapunto work involve working from the wrong side of a quilt, onto which a layer of open weave fabric has been fixed: cord and stuffing are introduced between the two layers, thereby raising these areas above the background of the quilt. In this way elaborate patterns can be created without the need to introduce any color.

The second type of early American quilt was the "medallion" quilt: vestiges of this convention can still be seen in contemporary quilts that are not either graphically representational or based on repeated blocks. A central motif or medallion dominates the quilt top and is emphasized by one or more borders that draw attention to and complement the main part of the design. These medallions were of skillful needlework executed in techniques and stitches originating in the places from where the colonists had emigrated, of *broderie perse*, or cut-out chintz work, in which chintz pieces were cut out and sewn onto the foundation fabric. At a time when lengths of fabric were highly prized, this was a way of making the most of a piece of material or, in some cases, rescuing something that had begun to wear out in places. Fabric producers were fully aware of how their products were used. Motifs and borders were printed specifically to be cut out, sometimes with a great many different borders being produced on one length of cloth. The main motif to be found on chintz was the flowing, twining form of a tree that sported fantastic flowers and fruit. This was a direct influence from the *palampores*, or stuffed chintz coverlets, that came from India and on which a favored design was the Tree of Life, sometimes showing the familiar paisley shape as the seed from which the tree sprang.

Influenced by such decorative elements, John Hewson, a famous Philadelphia printer, printed panels intended specifically for use as central medallions in quilt tops. Quilts bearing a medallion printed by him, with urns filled with flowers and beautiful fauna on branches, are now extremely sought after and increasingly rare. While both the wholecloth and medallion quilts persisted well into the early nineteenth century, toward the end of the eighteenth century, some quilts demonstrate a transition from the application of large areas of cut-out chintz to a newer method, where smaller motifs were brought together to create an entirely new design.

As the nineteenth century progressed, what we now know as "blockwork" increased in popularity to the extent that wholecloth and cut-out chintz quilts became a rarity, leaving mosaic piecework and blockwork as the types of quilt most often executed. Initially, mosaic blockwork revolved around the usual central medallion, with the borders of a formal medallion quilt being replaced by rows of pieced blocks. Toward the middle of the century, technology had progressed so far that the production of printed fabric had increased in speed and capacity providing a wide array of fabric for the domestic market. The country was opening up and transportation improving both for the movement of people and goods, and this affected quilting. For example, one explanation for the emergence and popularity of friendship quilts around the 1840s is the increased migration of people westward. A fashion arose for making quilts composed of blocks made by different people, often on the occasion of someone moving from one community to another. Sometimes the mail service was used to send blocks to a relation or friends who had already left. A variation on this was making mourning quilts, often using pieces of the deceased's garments. A modern-day revival of this habit of making mourning quilts is seen in the AIDS quilt (see page 101) which has captured the imagination of people internationally and done so much to raise the awareness of the need to prevent, rather than just cure, diseases.

As well as "friendship" quilts, other blockwork fashions included "signature" and "album" quilts. All these have similarities with one another and often the titles are used interchangeably though erroneously. In a signature

quilt, all the blocks are made from an identical design, though often in different fabrics and colors, and in some way the configuration of the blocks allows spaces for signatures. This space may be part of the block itself or, perhaps, a meeting point in the wide sashing that was often used to join the blocks together. An album or friendship quilt is made up of different blocks, either pieced, appliquéd, or a mixture of the two. The quilt may also be signed but not always in each block.

Another type of quilt could more accurately be called a "sampler" quilt. In much the same way as a young girl would make a needlework sampler to try out or show her prowess at a variety of stitches, so a quilter might experiment with new quilting blocks and quilting patterns.

Throughout the history of American quilt making, two main methods have remained constant: first, the piecing of different shapes, somewhat like a jigsaw, to produce a square or rectangular shape that can be joined with other similar blocks; second, a method of applying or appliquéing small or large motifs onto a background fabric. According to quilt historian Barbara Brackman, the availability of cheaper fabric—in the form of calico and cheaper machine-produced pins—allowed a wider range of women to produce intricately appliquéd quilts. From about

1830 the influence of the decorative art of German immigrants to Pennsylvania began to manifest itself in the design of appliquéd quilts. Motifs that were in evidence in other pieces of folk art, such as painted furniture, ceramics, and *Fraktur* paintings, began to transfer across to the quilts that were slowly being adopted as a type of bedcover by these Pennsylvanians of German origin.

This appliquéd style reached its zenith with the style that has become known as the "Baltimore album" quilt. This style of quilt combined the skills required for *broderie perse* with the variety of fabrics available toward the middle of the nineteenth century, and patterns and motifs from the various communities now settled in America. Complicated designs of vases, bowls, and baskets were filled to overflowing with vines, birds, fruits, and foliage built up in layers to produce shadows and contours. A favored configuration for a Baltimore album quilt was a grid of blocks either four rows of four or five rows of five. These blocks were usually delineated by strips of red sashing and completed with an appliquéd border of flowing vines and foliage. The predominant colors were red and green on a white background. A great many Baltimore album quilts were made during the period from 1846 to 1852 during the height of the fashion. It has been suggested that two Baltimore women, Achsah Goodwin Wilkins and Mary Evans, were responsible for a large number of these. In the case of Achsah Goodwin Wilkins this included the design of

the quilts, the direction of a group of young black girls, possibly even slaves, the provision of a place to quilt, and advice. Although genealogical evidence records the existence of a Mary Evans who married a John Ford in 1873, it has also been suggested (see Kiracofe, *The American Quilt*) that the name Mary Evans refers to a group of quilters rather than one individual—the number of quilts attributed to that name could never have been made by just one person.

The predominance of the color red in both these album quilts and other designs has already been remarked upon. Natural materials were the first substances used to change the color of cloth—such as insects and shellfish, and plants such as madder and indigo. Gradually, natural dyes began to be replaced by synthetics, the first colors being turkey red and a permanent green in 1810. Prior to this red was obtained either by the use of madder, which produced a brownish red, or from the cochineal beetle from Mexico or the Mediterranean shield louse. Cochineal had to be imported, and extremely large quantities were needed to dye a viable amount of cloth. Middle Eastern countries knew of a process that produced reds as bright as cochineal, but it was only in 1786 that Europeans succeeded in learning the process that yielded a bright and colorfast red dye. Once the "turkey red" secret had been discovered, it was in great demand, and despite a high price, was used extensively by quilters knowing that it provided them with a vibrant, colorfast dye. The equivalent, though still natural, blue was indigo. During

The combination of blue and white has always been popular in the decorative arts and has never really gone out of fashion as can be seen in this late twentieth century quilt. The quiltmaker has started with a mid-blue square, arranging pieces so that the ring of pieces gets progressively darker and then begins again with the lightest blue. © Roman Soumar/CORBIS

the nineteenth century, blue dye was made from woad, a substance extracted from the leaves of a plant that had been used by the Ancient Britons and extensively throughout Europe in the Middle Ages. The importance of woad decreased dramatically, however, as indigo began to be imported from India. The two plants share a colorfast substance, indigotin, that creates a blue coloring. However, in the Indian plant, *Indigofera tinctoria*, the substance is present in greater concentration than in the European plant, *Isatis tinctoria*. By the mid-eighteenth century, indigo, introduced to America by an enterprising young woman, Eliza Lucas Pinckney, was being grown in South Carolina and exported to England thus providing the English with a source of indigo from somewhere other than India. By obtaining indigo from India and America, the English were no longer dependent on the French as a source of woad for blue dye. The combination of blue and white has always been popular in the decorative arts, and by the second half of the nineteenth century, indigo and white was the color scheme most frequently chosen for a quilt. Both hand- and machine-woven coverlets made of indigo-dyed blue and white were available, and it seems likely that quiltmakers adapted these designs when they came to make their quilts.

Keen to discover a reason for the proliferation of this color scheme, some historians have linked the popularity of a combination of blue and white to the fact that these are the colors of the WCTU (Women's Christian Temperance Union). The society began in Ohio and was dedicated to making known the effect of alcohol on family life. Blue and white quilts have been found in large numbers in Ohio and a considerable number used the pattern "drunkard's path," but the more likely reason for a quilter using the color combination may merely be that blue was a lasting color and contrasted well with white.

As mentioned earlier, the availability of more reasonably priced fabric in a wide selection of patterns—with the added advantage of colorfast dyes—ensured that even more women were able to make piecework or patchwork quilts. The "log cabin" quilt falls somewhere in between pieced and appliquéd quilts. A log cabin block (see page 112) starts with an applied square, quite often in turkey red and said to represent the chimney of a log cabin. The overall effect of a log cabin quilt is that of a pieced patchwork quilt, achieved by the laying of one strip of fabric upon another to form a "square" or block, that is then pieced together to make a complete quilt. The many strips applied on top of one another add a textural appearance to the work, and so log cabin quilts are usually tied rather than being quilted. The number of patterns that can be created when making a log cabin quilt are only limited by the number of different ways in which the squares can be arranged, though the visual effect of a log cabin quilt can change drastically by the choice of fabrics and the combinations and contrasts that these stripped fabrics can achieve. All these variations of log cabin design achieve their end result by the ingenious arrangement of dark and light fabrics to create what amounts to an optical illusion. Log cabin may well have been one of the first forms of patchwork to emerge. The design is economical in the use of fabric: narrow strips of material, ribbon even, are used for this pattern, ensuring that even the smallest scraps of textile can be of some use. Each strip in a log cabin quilt is sewn separately onto the foundation fabric, and so unlike the making of other quilts, it is not essential that the quilt is made entirely of the same type of fabric. The foundation fabric ensures that the quilt retains its desired shape rather than being pulled out of alignment by the use of a mixture of materials. This mixture can see as diverse materials as silks, tweeds, worsteds, and velvet, all in the same quilt. It is probable that the quilts of the early settlers were constructed of just such "rag-bags" of component fabrics.

Superficially, one would never imagine that the "crazy" quilt had anything in common with the log cabin quilt other than the wide array of fabrics used within one quilt. However, although the shape of pieces used is different, the construction method is the same. One at a time, each piece of fabric is sewn onto a backing or foundation fabric with the preliminary stitching being extremely simple. While log cabin work uses the full potential of geometricity and regularity to achieve its final design, it is the apparent randomness of choice of fabrics and shapes that gives crazy patchwork its basic exotic appeal. However, unlike log cabin quilts, once the pieces have been applied onto each other, the quilt is not complete: a further layer, this time of embroidery, must be applied.

In 1876, America was exposed to the decorative art influences of Japan at the Centennial Exposition in Philadelphia. Just as the Great Exhibition in 1851 had proved so popular with the public of Victorian England, so the people of America took to the asymmetric principles of Japanese arts and crafts. Thus, the regular geometric designs of traditional block patterns were swept aside momentarily by this craze for crazy quilts. Oscar Wilde, one of the main proponents of the Aesthetic movement, toured the United States in 1882 and 1883. He often appeared at a lecture wearing a lily or a sunflower as a buttonhole, and both these flowers began to show up appliquéd and embroidered onto quilts.

Though the making of a crazy quilt provided an opportunity to incorporate pieces of cloth that evoked memories of people and events such as weddings and christenings, or even favorite garments, embroidery was as much a part of a crazy quilt as the snippets of precious fabrics such as silk and velvet. This embroidery was not confined to feather stitching along the seams between the various pieces of fabric. Elaborate motifs such as plants, animals, and birds were worked in thread that contrasted with the applied fabric pieces. So popular was this craze that it became possible to buy ready-made motifs to appliqué to crazy quilts. Commemorative ribbons gathered from political campaigns, horsefairs, and military and political campaigns were also included in these kaleidoscopic quilts. As the century closed, the crazy quilt craze came to an end—which is not to say that crazy quilts were never made after this date. Once a quilt pattern or theme has been introduced, it never quite disappears. Any quilting idea or pattern that is adopted by quilters is adapted to local, technical, or contemporary needs and is absorbed into the quilting repertoire.

A great deal of thought and creativity went into designing of quilts. They certainly were not merely a way of using up left-over fabric; indeed, as has already been stated, a vast number of quilts were never intended for daily use. The overall plan of some quilts depended so heavily on having the right amount of each color fabric that it had to be purchased specially. This type of quilt is often referred to as a "show" quilt: it would never have gone anywhere near anyone's bed and was made purely for decoration, even if the place of display was an unused bed.

The largest show quilt, indeed, the largest quilt of any type ever constructed, is the AIDS Memorial Quilt. This project is a work in progress that came into existence in 1985. Observing marchers arranging cards with the names of AIDS victims, Cleve Jones, a gay rights campaigner, initiated a memorial of greater longevity. Commemorative patches are sewn together into panels measuring three feet by six feet. As well as providing the traditional purpose of commemoration and healing, as did nineteenth century quilts made from clothes of the deceased, this quilt has also proved to be the focus of highly successful health education programs and a source of fund-raising for research into a devastating disease.

It may seem alien for the genteel world of quilting to be disrupted by politics, but the quilt has provided a means of supporting various causes. During the middle of the nineteenth century, quilts made specifically for fund-raising were auctioned in aid of political or philanthropic causes. The most common method of raising money was by charging people to have their signatures added to the quilt, which was then auctioned to raise further funds. In appearance these quilts hardly varied from those made as friendship quilts. For example, more women than men are thought to have been members of antislavery societies: they made use of their needle skills to raise funds for their beliefs. In keeping with the position of women at the time, their efforts may not have been as noticeable as women of later times. Other than embroidering phrases such as, "may the points of our needles prick the slave owner's conscience," women had to content themselves with renaming familiar quilting patterns: new names that emerged were "underground railway," "slave chain," and "North Star" quilts. Stories are told of quilts being used as signals of safe houses for slaves on the run. Since universal suffrage, the position of women has changed so much that in 1987, in the Crystal Court of Philip Johnson's IDS Building in Minneapolis, 430 women were able to take part in a piece of performance art by Suzanne Lacy entitled "The Crystal Quilt." Viewers from the balconies of the court had a bird's eye view of older women, dressed in black costumes, sitting at tables for four. To a soundtrack that combined the natural sounds of

This group of elderly women, photographed on January 1, 1962, have gathered together for a quilting bee in Fort Lauderdale to sew quilts for the needy. They are seen quilting a top with alternating plain blocks and a design known as "Sunbonnet Sue." This design features a girl with her face obscured by a large sunbonnet, and first appeared in the 1920s. As with most quilting designs, this one has remained in the quilter's repertoire. The frame on which these Fort Lauderdale women are working is supported from beneath.
© Bettmann/CORBIS

Minnesota with voices in conversation and the statement of Meridel LeSueur, the eighty-year old female activist, "I am not aging, I'm ripening," a choreographed unfolding of black table covers began. In formation, the seated women unfolded the dark table covers to reveal cloths of red and yellow. The effect was of a living, breathing, pieced quilt.

While twentieth century artists have seized upon the graphic qualities and communal possibilities provided by quilts and quilting, a group of people who are famous for shunning modern life have succeeded in making their version of the craft immediately recognizable. At first glance Amish quilts would appear to be simple in design. They are usually made up of three main shapes— rectangles, squares, and triangles. Almost without exception, Amish quilts use no shapes or pieces that do not have straight edges. However, the quilting used to attach the quilt tops to the filling and the backing is often as elaborate as the piecing on non-Amish quilts. Suggestions have been made that Amish women's choice of shapes was restricted by the *Ordnung*, or strict rules of behavior of their religious group, and their complicated quilting was an attempt to break away from these rules. This idea seems somewhat ludicrous: though the elders of the group would have been male, this does not preclude them from noticing what they might well consider to be frivolous, unacceptable designs.

More believable is that the configuration of many quilts is based on something that would have been present in every Amish home, the *Ausbund* or Amish hymnal. Up until and including the nineteenth century, these Ausbunds were bound in leather with raised ornamentations of brass at the corners and some central brass shape in the center, often a diamond. In turn these brass bosses were embossed with further decoration. The leather of the Ausbunds was tooled with patterns sharing motifs and characteristics that can be compared with Amish quilting patterns. It is not unreasonable to surmise that, just as ceramics, textiles, and wall coverings influenced other women's quilt designs, so the Amish women, consciously or subconsciously, made use of the decorative elements that they came across in their daily lives. To the eyes of nineteenth century viewers, the solid colors of the Amish quilts may have seemed unbearably plain and old-fashioned as they resembled, to a great degree, the wholecloth quilts of the first settlers. However, those who have been exposed to the influences of abstract artists in the twentieth century may find the blocks of color in Amish quilts refreshingly modern. Unfettered by choices of emblem, motif, or block pattern, Amish quiltmakers were able to concentrate on what quilt writers Robert Bishop and Elizabeth Safanda refer to in *Amish Quilts* as "the dynamics of tension and release." The prime concern of the quilter has been the manner in which the large shapes and the deep, solid, unpatterned colors work together. Amish quilts have also been spoken of in terms of reflecting the "sunshine and shadow" of living a rural, and to the eyes of outsiders, primitive life.

In 1971 the Whitney Museum in New York was the venue for an exhibition entitled "American Pieced Quilts."

When access to a quilt is required by a number of quilters, an alternative to supporting the frame from beneath is to hang it from the ceiling as is the case with the frame of these Women of the Supply Community, in Brunswick County, North Carolina. Both this and the frame seen on page 17 appear to be no wider than a kitchen or dining table. © Bettmann/CORBIS

This exhibition was the starting point for a revival of interest in quilting that gathered momentum as the century progressed. The bicentennial of 1976 stirred up interest in everything traditionally American and provided subject matter and symbols for this commemorative opportunity. Once again, communities and organizations felt spurred into creating something to celebrate their local ties. To some practitioners of the craft of quilting, this so-called revival would have been no surprise, for quilting had never completely disappeared.

The quilting party or quilting "bee" brought together a group of women with the primary aim of completing a quilt. It would appear that there was an acceptance that a woman would not wish to or even, perhaps, could not complete a quilt on her own. This in no way seemed to suggest that a woman who could not undertake the making of a quilt from planning, through collecting the cloth and piecing to the final stages of quilting, was inadequate. On the contrary, it has always been accepted practice for some to have their tops quilted by someone else. Ruby Short McKim, who compiled *101 Patchwork Patterns* in 1931, suggests that after the top has been pieced together, "It is usually the wisest thing here to call upon a professional quilter or your church 'aid society' to complete the task—especially if you are inexperienced and the quilt top handsome." She continues by explaining how prices for quilting vary, dependent on the amount of quilting work to be found in an area, the standard of the quilting required, and the amount of thread used. McKim

quotes prices ranging from 75 cents to $5.00 for a spool of thread. McKim also acknowledges the changes in lifestyle taking place in the first half of the twentieth century and suggests a manner of "apartment" or "compartment" quilting that does not entail the use of a frame.

By the end of the twentieth century it might be said that there were four separate strands to quilt making. First, the traditional quilt school remains primarily in the domestic sphere, with women reusing and adapting old patterns while eagerly incorporating modern materials and tools into their craft. This part of quilt making also encompasses the proliferation of classes, shops, and associated businesses that quilting now supports. Not only are fabrics and patterns produced for quilters, technology has now moved beyond the electric sewing machine with the introduction of computer programs.

Second, the quilt is still used politically—today for the advancement of causes such as feminism and world awareness of issues such as AIDS.

Third, the history of quilts is studied as art and the consequent use of such quilts as a social history tool to uncover the lives of ordinary people, particularly women, in what has been called "hidden history" or "history from below." As with oral history, the study of a quilt can provide significant clues to the daily life of individuals, families, or social groups.

Finally, the quilt has achieved acceptance as a high art form with the term "fiber art" being created to cover such works.

The quilt has never stopped evolving. While traditionalists attempt to preserve patterns and techniques and spurn any aid or tool that they consider inappropriate, there are others taking the art forward in leaps and bounds, not least the artists who have appropriated quilting as a means of affirming their gender and their heritage.

AFRICAN-AMERICAN QUILTS

The vital contributions to American cultural life made by African-Americans in fields such as music have long been recognized, but it is only in the years since 1970 that serious critical and scholarly attention has been focused on their role in the visual arts. Despite the cultural flowering of the Harlem Renaissance in the 1920s and the individual success of artists such as Jacob Lawrence and Romare Bearden, African-American art has struggled to gain acceptance. In recent decades, however, scholars have reappraised many aspects of African-American visual culture, and in the process identified and documented distinctive styles and traits. Building on the pioneering research of Robert Farris Thompson, a Professor in the Art History Department at Yale, attention has been particularly focused on the extent to which these styles and traits may be traceable back to African antecedents. Folk art by African-Americans, which previous generations of scholars had ignored or at best regarded as minor curios derived from mainstream white American forms, is now, with the benefit of a deeper understanding of African art, seen to display numerous apparent continuities with African traditions. This raises questions about the transmission of culture and aesthetics that are fascinating, if hard to answer.

Many African-American quilts share features which, taken together, have been seen to distinguish them from other American quilting traditions, and to show demonstrable similarities with aspects of textile design in Africa. In a few recent cases the quilters have been sophisticated artists with a fine art education deliberately exploring the resonance of their sense of African heritage. More usually, however, the quilts are the work of rural women with little or no knowledge of African textiles. The study of African-American quilting is dominated by the research of Maude Southwell Wahlman, whose book *Signs and Symbols* is a highly informative overview of the field. As we will see, Wahlman has identified five aesthetic principles, which she regards as demonstrating continuity with African textile design. In addition there are numerous signs and symbols particularly apparent in appliqué quilts, which may have been handed on from generation to generation long after their explicit meaning, had been forgotten. Before we look at these apparent aesthetic and cultural continuities, we will take a brief look at the history of African-American quilting and introduce a few of the best known quilters of the twentieth century.

Unfortunately, very little is known about earlier phases of African-American quilting as the earliest securely dated and provenanced pieces to survive are a few from the nineteenth century. Nevertheless it seems clear that slave women both sewed quilts for use in the "big house" and used scraps of calico and other material along with salvaged flour sacks and the like to create quilts for their own families. Women quickly adapted and "creolized" a tradition of European origin to meet their own tastes and needs. A number of these so-called "slave quilts" from early in the nineteenth century survive in museum collections and provide an important early source for scholars. By far the best-known and most discussed African-American quilts also date from the nineteenth century. These are the two "Bible quilts" made by Harriet Powers, now in the Smithsonian National Museum of American History and the Museum of Fine Arts, Boston.

Harriet Powers was born in slavery in Georgia in October 1837. By the 1880s she was married with two children, the family owning a small farm in Clarke County, near Athens, Georgia. Harriet supplemented the farm income by working as a seamstress, allowing her to support herself after her husband left in 1895. She died in 1911. Harriet Powers has achieved posthumous fame for two remarkable quilts, each illustrating biblical scenes, accompanied in the second quilt by illustrations of strange celestial events. The first quilt, now in the Smithsonian, was shown at cotton fair in Athens in 1886. Using a vivid and assured appliqué technique, Powers depicted eleven bible scenes from the Garden of Eden to the Nativity, each scene separated and framed by sashing. Powers refused an offer to buy the quilt from a local art teacher, but was obliged by poverty to sell it five years later. Fortunately, she

gave the buyer a detailed account of the iconography, which was recorded and amplified in a lengthy letter. Soon afterward, Powers began work on a second, more elaborate, quilt. Once again Powers was obliged by poverty to sell her work, in this case after it was shown in the Nashville Exposition of 1898. It was purchased by the faculty wives of Atlanta University and given to the chairman of the university board of trustees. Its importance even at the time is apparent as much from this prestige destination as the fact that, once again, Powers' explanation of her imagery was recorded. This quilt has fifteen scenes, several of which depict unusual celestial events apparently regarded as having symbolic significance. For example the second square shows the "dark day of May 19, 1780" caused by smoke from forest fires.

Although appliqué quilt making was an established tradition in the South, the striking visual similarity between Mrs. Powers' masterpieces and certain African textile techniques, and the focus on celestial themes have given rise to considerable academic debate about the extent of African influence in the two quilts. There are certainly close visual similarities between the figures in the quilts and those found in appliqué banners made for the royal court of Dahomey in the Benin Republic, as well as the appliqué flags of the Fante of coastal Ghana. However, it seems improbable that there can be more than a very indirect and tenuous connection between the two. More intriguing is the emphasis on cosmological imagery, given the artist's stated intention to "preach the gospel in patchwork, to show my lord my humility." The only known picture of Harriet Powers shows her wearing an apron embroidered with a small cross and two stars or suns similar to those in the quilts. Whether or not this supports the speculation of some scholars that Mrs. Powers may have had Masonic links or been a "conjure woman," it doesn't seem unreasonable to suppose that her interest in the stars reflected their importance in African-derived folk traditions still widespread among rural African-Americans at the end of the nineteenth century.

However, Harriet Powers' work was actually located in a wider tradition. From our perspective she stands out as an exceptional figure in the history of African-American quilting, known and remembered because the virtuosity of her art was sufficiently recognized for her identity and even her explanations to be recorded. This was not the case with most other early quilters, although sufficient examples of nineteenth century quilting do survive for design continuities to be apparent. It was only with increasing interest in the 1970s, and the research by Maude Southwell Wahlman and others that followed, that the names, opinions, and life histories of other quilters were systematically recorded and due recognition began to be given to their achievements. Inevitably, these were mostly rather elderly ladies who were still active quilters in the second half of the twentieth century. Among the best known are Mozell Benson, Arester Earl, Nora Ezell, Mary Maxtion, Martha Jane Pettway (born 1898) and her three daughters Plummer T, Leola, and Joanna Pettway, Pearlie

Posey, Lucinda Toomer, and Pecolia Warner. Typically they learned to quilt as a child by watching and assisting their mother or grandmother. Quilting was a social activity in the old rural South. In an interview with Pearlie Posey, who was born on a Mississippi plantation, Dr. Wahlman recorded the following comments that capture a now remote lifestyle:

> "*When the sun went down, you could take your mule out and go on home and feed your mule, and if it was still light, why you could sit down and quilt two or three, a few rows.*
> "*In my time, would be a family there and a family there and a family there and we would get together and tear up old clothes, overalls, and linings and everything and piece quilt tops and linings.*"

By the 1980s women were still making quilts at home for their families but many were also members of a quilting bee. By that time also, for a few women of later generations, their quilting heritage had been transformed into a fine art medium through which stories about issues such as race and cultural identity could be explored from a feminist perspective. Faith Ringgold and Joyce Scott are the best-known artists using quilts as a narrative medium in a way that harks back to Harriet Powers' Bible quilts.

So what is African about African-American quilt making? Although quilts as such were not made in Africa, there are quite a number of patchwork and appliqué textile

THE ART OF THE QUILT

traditions. Patchwork was found in Sudanese robes, Kuba and "pygmy" bark cloth in Central Africa, Yoruba Egungun masquerade costumes, and perhaps the most markedly similar to quilt tops, in the war robes worn by chiefs of people such as the Loma and Gola in western Liberia.

Appliqué traditions include Kuba raffia cloth, Cameroon grass field robes, and Ibibio funerary shrines, in addition to the Fante Asafo flags and Fon banners already mentioned. However, direct continuity with any of these is quite unlikely. More probable is that when slave women began to quilt from European prototypes, and in particular when they sewed quilts for their own use, their work was informed by memories of African cloth styles. Given the huge numbers of people involved in textile production in precolonial West Africa, it is even likely that many plantations had slaves with direct experience of the trade. It is not clear whether any African cloth or weaving techniques were present in the early period of slavery in North America, although this is not inconceivable, as both have been documented in Brazil. At any event cloth was a highly valued commodity and most people had a good knowledge of types made in or imported into their locality, which all slaves born in Africa would have shared.

Evidence that African-American quilting was informed by African cloth making traditions is apparent in certain shared aesthetic principles (Wahlman & Scully, 1983), and perhaps also in the presence of signs and symbols of African origin (Wahlman, 1993). Five key aesthetic principles have been noted: the use of strips,

large-scale designs, high color contrast, offbeat patterns, and multiple rhythms. It should be stressed that both African textiles and African-American quilts are highly varied and not all these features are found in all examples. Nevertheless it is suggested that they are sufficiently widespread to be characteristic features.

Much, although by no means all, African cloth is woven on looms that produce narrow strips around four to six inches in width, which are then sewn together edge to edge. There can be no doubt that many centuries of this tradition have made it a widely shared aesthetic preference in much of West Africa, with numerous examples known where wider loom cloth has been woven to imitate narrow strips, and of imported fabric being cut into strips and resewn. A similar sensibility has been documented in the Americas where the Maroons, descendants of escaped African slaves living in the rainforests of Surinam (on the north coast of South America), cut up factory cloth into strips before resewing it as patchwork cloaks. Many African-American quilters also used strips of cloth, either as a whole piece, or sewn together from numerous small rectangular scraps, known as strings, to structure and organize quilt tops. This is a feature only rarely seen in quilting of Euro-American origin.

Although many African textiles such as kente do have small and intricate motifs, these are usually set within a large-scale overall design visible at a distance. Similarly, and in contrast to most other American quilts, African-American quilts are often dominated by a single large pattern. Like certain African fabrics, such as the "checkerboard" blankets found in Mali and Burkina Faso, African-American quilters often display a marked preference for bright, contrasting colors. Pecolia Warner spoke of choosing colors that "hit" each other in an interview with Maude Wahlman. Both strong colors and large-scale patterns are used in a complex, improvisational way to create effects that have been described as "off-beat" patterns and "multiple rhythms." Both are features that, drawing on the parallels between jazz and African music, Robert Farris Thompson argues are characteristic of African textile design. This quality is well described by Wahlman (1983), "The effect of these constant improvisations with color is to double, triple, and fragment patterns and rhythms so that one can see multiple accents which disrupt and suspend any regular flow of movement with color or form."

While visual similarities are readily perceived, identifying signs and symbols of African ancestry is a more complex problem, in part because we are dealing mostly with simple forms such as crosses, squares, hands, and circles which are found with varying significance in many cultural contexts. There is no doubt that there were many complex and nuanced systems of signs and quasi-scripts in precolonial Africa, including Asante adinkra cloth motifs, Vai and Ejagham scripts, and Kongo cosmograms. It is also

well documented that elements of secret scripts of Kongolese and other African origins were and still are known in the Americas in the context of Afro-Caribbean religious systems such as Haitian Vodoun and Cuban Santeria. In Kongo cosmograms, and in many other African traditions, a cross or crossroads could mark a point of transition between the world of the living and that of the ancestral dead. This belief, cited by Robert Johnson and countless other blues singers who "went down to the crossroads," clearly lived on in African-American folk traditions. Similarly, one common form of charm or "mojo" in the South was a red cloth square. Colors may have had symbolic resonances, as they certainly did in much of Africa, while complex and broken patterns might protect by diverting or interrupting the flow if malevolent spirits. Most twentieth century quilters would no longer have placed such precise interpretations on their work, although they may have been echoing a tradition whose content has been forgotten. On the other hand maybe they are just colors, just shapes. It is unlikely we will ever know for certain. Nevertheless, scholars from Zora Neale Hurston to Robert Farris Thompson and Maude Wahlman have performed a valuable and fascinating service in documenting and speculating about the often hidden "Africanisms" in African-American culture. It is certainly more interesting to look at the quilts from that perspective.

TREE OF LIFE WHITEWORK QUILT

By an unidentified maker, this quilt, made of cotton with a cotton fringe, is prominently dated 1796. An indication of the orientation of the quilt is given by the central third of the top edge being unfringed, and by the orientation and placing of the date in the center foot of the quilt. Apart from these small indications, it might initially be assumed that the pattern on this whitework bedspread is symmetrical; this is not the case. Closer inspection reveals some anomalies that might suggest that the maker or designer had observed the growth patterns of plants. The relief effect is achieved by cording the linear elements and padding the larger areas such as leaves and fruit: this is known as trapunto work.

Tree of Life Whitework Quilt

* Quiltmaker unidentified, United States; 1796
* Cotton with cotton fringe
* height 92¼" width 87¾"
* Collection of the American Folk Art Museum, New York
  Gift of Cyril Irwin Nelson in honor of Joel and
  Kate Kopp
  1997.16.1

CALIMANCO QUILT WITH BORDER

As with so many quilts, the maker of this wool wholecloth quilt in two strong shades of blue, is unknown. The design of the quilt could hardly be simpler. Constructed of dark solid fabric quilted all over in a fine regular pattern of diagonal lines, the only relief from a solid expanse of single cloth is that the border is of a darker tone than the main part of the quilt. The top edge of the quilt that would have been covered with pillows has no border, demonstrating the thought that went into the planning of a quilt as an item with a useful purpose, even when it was kept for show rather than being used every day.

Calimanco Quilt with Border

* Quiltmaker unidentified, United States; 1810–20
* Glazed wool
* height 96" width 91"
* Collection of the American Folk Art Museum, New York
* Gift of Cyril Irwin Nelson in devoted memory of his grandmother, Elinor Irwin (Chase) Holden
  1993.6.5 Photo by Scott Bowron

HARLEQUIN MEDALLION QUILT

This strikingly geometric quilt is from New England. The regular angled echo quilting that follows the shape of the triangles is relieved slightly by a strip of arced quilting lines around the central blocked top of the quilt. The doubling-up of blocks in the center of the quilt is an interesting method of emphasizing the dimensions of the bed on which the quilt will be spread. The quilt has the characteristic shiny gloss of fabric that has been calendared. The effect of this process, in which a rotary iron process is used, is particularly noticeable and effective in the black and red portions of fabric. The overall design bears a passing resemblance to designs and colors that have come to be thought typical of Amish quilting. However, as vibrant and strong as this quilt is, it does not quite achieve the heights of color combination inherent in most Amish quilts.

Harlequin Medallion Quilt

* Quiltmaker unidentified, New England; 1800–20
* Glazed wool
* height 87" width 96"
* Collection of the American Folk Art Museum, New York
* Gift of Cyril Irwin Nelson in loving memory of his grandparents John Williams and Sophie Anna Macy 1984.33.1

APPLIQUÉD AND EMBROIDERED PICTORIAL BEDCOVER

By an unidentified maker, possibly from New York, this bedcover of wool, silk and cotton and beads with silk and cotton embroidery is a show quilt: it was never intended for everyday use. The appliquéd animals, flowers, and leaves are of silk sewn onto a fine wool background. This quilt is similar in configuration to wholecloth quilts discussed earlier: large expanses of solid colored cloth are employed with the decoration emanating from a central medallion. However, in this case, decoration is not provided by cut-out purpose-printed chintz and elaborate quilting patterns but by motifs designed by the maker and cut-out in silk. There is no decorative quilting at all: any interest is provided by the richness and color of the silk pieces alone.

Appliquéd and Embroidered Pictorial Bedcover

* Maker unidentified, possibly New York; 1825–45
* Wool, silk, cotton, and beads with silk and cotton embroidery
* height 87" width 86"
* Collection of the American Folk Art Museum, New York
* Gift of Ralph Esmerian 1991.27.1

MARTHA MICOU CUT-OUT CHINTZ QUILT

This almost perfectly square quilt, made by Martha Micou, is almost certainly made from chintz printed specifically to be used for cut-out chintz work. Even the border around the central medallion would have been made for just such a purpose. These prints were based on the palampores (from the town of Palanpur in the Gujarat region of India) or bedspreads that came out of India to England in the sixteenth century, and then later to America. Various origins of the word chintz have been suggested from the Hindi chitta, meaning spotted, or "chint" said to mean variegated. Whatever the origin, these palampores and the cloth based on their designs utilized many colors in complicated depictions of exotic plants, flowers, and birds. Made between 1835 and 1840 this quilt is typical of the time: the design consists of a large central medallion surrounded by several "rings" of cut-out chintz or broderie perse.

Martha Micou Cut-Out Chintz Quilt

* Martha Chatfield Micou, possibly Virginia or South Carolina; 1835–40
* Cotton
* height 92" width 92½"
* Collection of the American Folk Art Museum, New York
* Gift of Mary W. Carter
  1988.2.1 Photo by Matt Hoebermann

VARIABLE STARS QUILT

This cotton and linen New England quilt combines two types of quilt design: an appliquéd, cut-out chintz or broderie perse center; with the remainder of the quilt being pieced chintz. This quilt uses a wide variety of printed fabrics suggesting that the maker may have saved pieces for a considerable time before commencing the quilt, though often quilters would exchange with friends and relations to increase the range of their pieces. Around 1790, prints on a dark background became fashionable and were often printed in strips ready for quiltmakers to cut out for borders. The fabric used for the central star, the medallion border and the two external borders may well have been made of such textiles. There are three clues that assist with the dating of this quilt: the transitory method that combines broderie perse with piecing; the extensive use of prints with a darker ground; and the saw-tooth or zig-zag style border that, according to quilt writer Barbara Brackman, is "rarely seen after 1850."

Variable Stars Quilt

* Quiltmaker unidentified, New England; 1825–40
* Cotton and linen
* height 95" width 87"
* Collection of the American Folk Art Museum, New York
* Purchase made possible by the George and Frances Armour Foundation
  1985.33.1 Photo by Matt Hoebermann

SARAH MORRELL ALBUM QUILT

This quilt is made of cotton with signatures of ink with cotton embroidery, and bears the name "Sarah Morrell" in the center medallion. The combination of the central medallion with pieced blocks and a saw-tooth border on three sides of the quilt all corroborate the assumed date of this piece, around 1843. Fifty-eight people, both male and female, signed the quilt but as yet no definite ties have been established between the signatories. The quilt is predominantly red and white with each block different. However, despite the wide range of blocks incorporated, the overall design is well balanced with pieced blocks alternating with those of cut-out chintz. The use of a double saw-tooth border around the central medallion and around the majority of the pieced blocks serves to link the main part of the quilt with what was originally a red saw-tooth border.

Sarah Morrell Album Quilt

* Possibly Sarah Morrell and others, Pennsylvania and New Jersey; 1843
* Cotton and ink with cotton embroidery
* height 93¼" width 95¼"
* Collection of the American Folk Art Museum, New York
* Gift of Jeremy L. Banta
  1986.16.1 Photo by Schecter Lee

SAVERY FRIENDSHIP STAR QUILT

The majority of the signatories on this friendship quilt came from central Philadelphia and Chester County, Pennsylvania. Research by Mimi Sherman, for the American Folk Art Museum, has proved many of them to be closely related. The central star is signed by "EHS," for Elizabeth Hooten (Cresson) Savery, with the signatures of her husband, mother, and mother-in-law being close by. The quilt is made of cotton and linen, with inked signatures and drawings, and dates from 1844. In the 1830s a permanent ink, that didn't damage fabric, was developed: this led to a great fashion for making signature quilts. The extended family represented in this quilt were Quakers: studies by quilt historian Jessica Nicoll reveal that they eschewed the more lively variety of colors and block patterns, in sampler album quilts, in favor of more uniform sober designs as demonstrated in this quilt.

Savery Friendship Star Quilt

* Elizabeth Hooten (Cresson) Savery and others, Philadelphia; 1844
* Cotton and linen with inked signatures and drawings
* height 80" width 83¼"
* Collection of the American Folk Art Museum, New York
* Gift of Marie D. and Charles A. T. O'Neill
  1979.26.1 Photo by Matt Hoebermann

FEATHERED
TOUCHING STARS QUILT

This cotton quilt, dated 1846 and made in Ohio, is similar in design to the previous one though this is made from sixteen identical large pieced blocks. There is no border, it is simply finished off with thin red binding. These feathered star designs were not to be undertaken by an inexperienced quilter: care was needed to ensure that pieces did not become distorted or puckered when sewn together. In a pieced quilt, such as this one of feathered touching stars, the fabric elements are seamed together whereas in an appliquéd quilt, one piece of fabric is sewn upon another.

Feathered Touching Stars Quilt

* Quiltmaker unidentified, Ohio; 1846
* Cotton
* height 85½" width 84¾"
* Collection of the American Folk Art Museum, New York
* Gift of Cyril Irwin Nelson
  1989.17.6 Photo by Matt Hoebermann

PIETIES QUILT

Maria Cadman Hubbard was born in 1769: this cotton quilt of hers was probably made in 1848 in Austerlitz, Columbia County, New York. The entire quilt is of turkey red and white. Maria Cadman Hubbard has used both the color scheme and piecing configuration to great effect. Apart from two areas where she has pieced her name, age, and year that the quilt was made, each large white area proclaims a "piety." These quotations are spelled out in geometric red and white which together with the remainder of the quilt being executed in saw-tooth piecing achieve an effect akin to an optical illusion. The quilt is dated 1848, two years before the date that writer Barbara Brackman suggests the saw-tooth or zig-zag borders declined in popularity.

Pieties Quilt

* Maria Cadman Hubbard (c. 1769–?),
  probably Austerlitz, Columbia County, New York; 1848
* Cotton
* height 88½" width 81"
* Collection of the American Folk Art Museum, New York
* Gift of Cyril Irwin in loving memory of his parents,
  Cyril Arthur and Elise Macy Nelson
  1984.27.1 Photo by Matt Hoebermann

Little acts of kindness
Little words of love

Make our earthly eden
like our Heaven above

Is our
Home a
Heaven

Heaven
is our
Home

Peace Be still

Kind
words
Never
Die

Forgive
as you
hope to be
Forgiven

Earth has
no sorrow
Heaven
cannot
heal

Be still
and know
that I am
God

No Cross No Crown

Thy Will be done

Oh sacred
Patience
with my
soul abide

There is a
magic in
kindness
that springs
from above

Maria
Cadman
Hubbard
aged 79

If you can
not be a
Golden Pipp
and don't turn
crab apple

abide with us

Love one
another

1848

MARINER'S COMPASS QUILT

This striking pieced quilt was made by an unidentified quiltmaker in the later part of the nineteenth century—circa 1880-1890. Initials—BB, possibly those of the maker—are embroidered in ornate capitals in opposite corners of the quilt, but, sadly, we do not know who BB was, other than that he or she lived in Maine and was obviously interested in the sea. The radiating points mimic those found on a compass—thus the name—and the maritime theme is taken up in the dark blue material that has anchors printed on it in white. One of two Mariner's Compass quilts in the collection of the Museum of American Folk Art in New York City, this style dates back into the eighteenth century.

Mariner's Compass Quilt

* Quiltmaker unidentified, United States; 1840-1860
* Cotton
* height 75¼" width 70"
* Collection of the American Folk Art Museum, New York
* Gift of Kinuko Fujii, Osaka, Japan
  1991.8.2 Photo by Matt Hoebermann

APPLIQUÉ CRIB QUILT

Dating from 1840 to 1869 and probably from Pennsylvania, this cotton quilt by an unidentified maker was obviously intended for use on a crib. The quilt has a naive appearance with much in common with quilts making the transition from wholecloth to cut-out chintz. However, in this quilt rather than a small medallion and a large expanse of cloth, the medallion has "exploded" until it nearly reaches the edges of the quilt. The outer fabric is a dark paisley design with the appliquéd parts on the main area of the quilt of cotton with a darker ground. There is no saw-tooth border, which was rarely seen after 1840, but instead the dividing line, between the dark paisley border and the ground on which the shapes are appliquéd, is castellated. The effect is similar to cookie-cutter quilts where biscuit cutter shapes served as inspiration, perhaps even as templates.

Appliqué Crib Quilt

* Quiltmaker unidentified, probably Pennsylvania; 1840–60
* Cotton
* height 33¼" width 33¾" framed
* Collection of the American Folk Art Museum, New York
* Gift of Joel and Kate Kopp
  1980.5.1 Photo by Scott Bowron

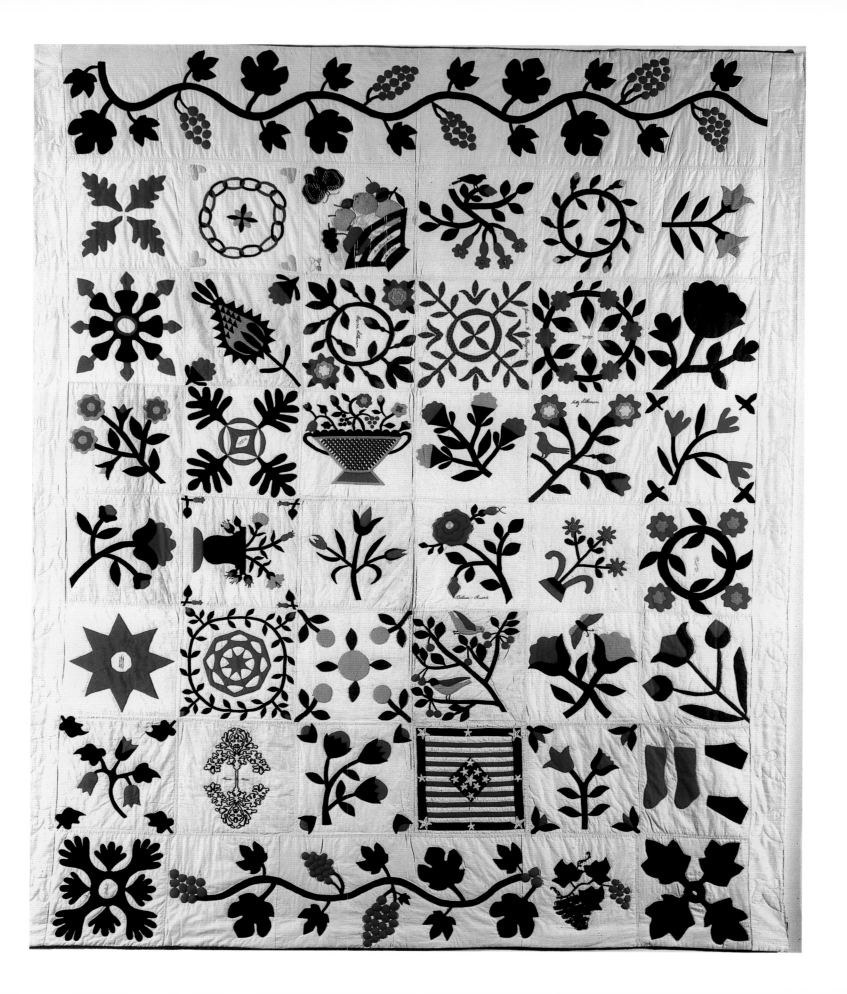

CROSS RIVER ALBUM QUILT

This cotton and silk quilt with wool embroidery from Cross River, New York was made in 1861 by Mrs. Eldad Miller (1805–74) and others. It is a fine example of a sampler or album quilt with blocks being made on a white ground with all the appliqué being in the popular color combination of red, green, and yellow, apart from one square. This may commemorate the start of the Civil War in 1861 and suggests the allegiance of the makers of the quilt. Research by Paula Laverty at the American Folk Art Museum has discovered that all the contributors to the quilt lived within a few miles of each other and were between the ages of fifteen and fifty-five. The quilt displays a wide range of techniques, designs and abilities, suggesting that the quilters may have used the construction of such an album quilt to experiment with new ideas and methods before they proceeded to larger projects of their own.

Cross River Album Quilt

* Mrs. Eldad Miller and others, Cross River, New York; 1861
* Cotton and silk with wool embroidery
* height 90" width 75"
* Collection of the American Folk Art Museum, New York
* Gift of Dr. Stanley and Jacqueline Schneider 1980.8.1 Photo by Gavin Ashworth

MARY JANE SMITH LOG CABIN QUILT, BARN RAISING VARIATION

This magnificent log cabin quilt, of cotton, wool, and silk, was made by two women of a prosperous farming family: Mary Jane Smith (1833–69); and her mother, Mary Morrell Smith (1798–1869) of Whitestone, Queen's County, New York between the years 1861–65. As well as being the oldest log cabin quilt in the collection of the American Folk Art Museum, it is supported by full documentation of its history. The quilt was intended as part of the young woman's trousseau, but tragedy struck. The bridegroom died of pneumonia the day before the wedding and the bride three years later: the quilt was never used. The configuration of the log cabin blocks ably demonstrates the care needed to order and arrange the scraps used in such a quilt. In each block the dark fabrics occupy one diagonal half, opposed by the light strips.

Log Cabin Quilt,
Barn Raising Variation

* Mary Jane Smith (1833–69) and Mary Morrell Smith (1798–69), Whitestone, Queens County, New York; 1861–65
* Cotton, wool and silk
* height 81" width 74"
* Collection of the American Folk Art Museum, New York
* Gift of Mary D. Bromham, grandniece of Mary Jane Smith 1987.9.1 Photo by Schecter Lee

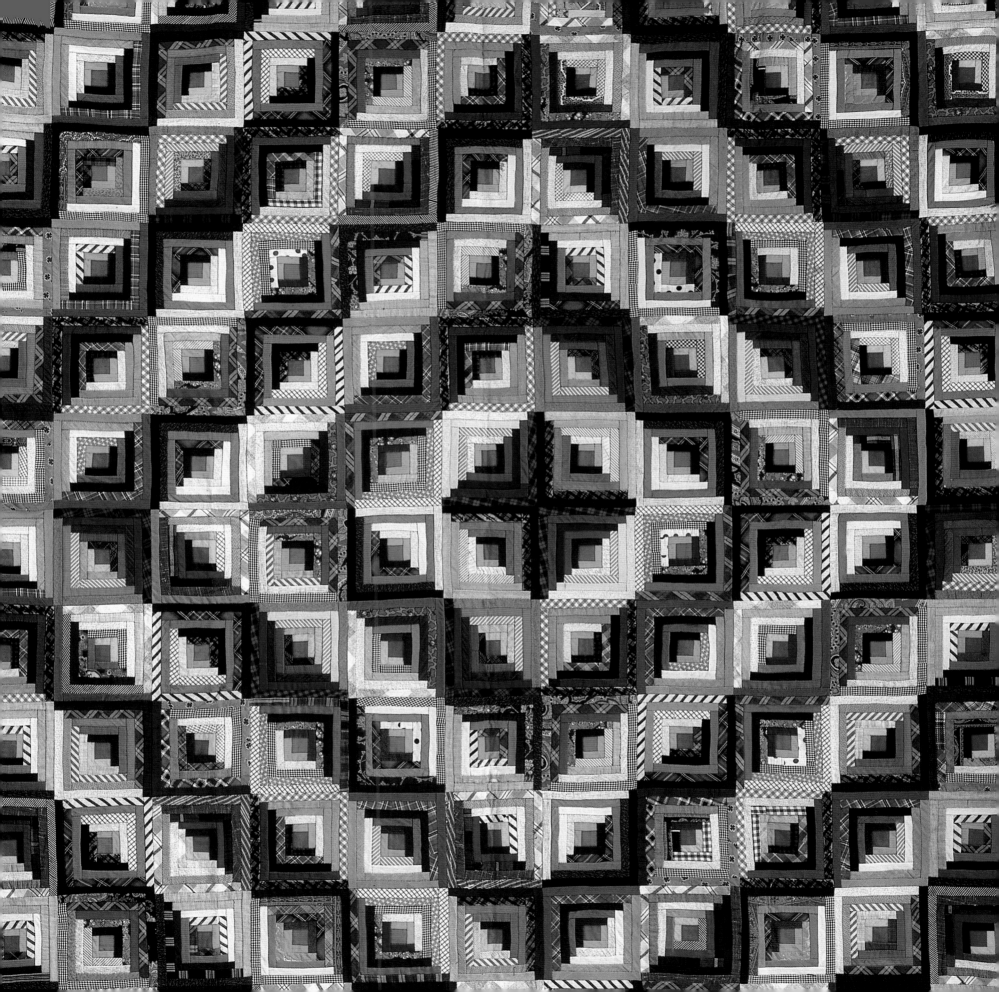

ECB FEATHERED STAR QUILT

Blue and white is a color scheme that occurs regularly throughout all areas of decorative art. Around 1840 this combination increased in popularity in quilting, however, this cotton pieced quilt dates from one or two decades later. Though the maker of the quilt is unidentified, it bears the pieced initials "ECB"—possibly the maker's. The main part of the quilt has been cleverly arranged from thirty-five blocks in three different designs. Around this configuration of blocks is a frame of half-blocks. The final border is of blue plant forms appliquéd onto the white ground. It has been suggested that these blue and white quilts were heavily influenced by coverlets that were made of indigo blue wool woven into white cotton or linen. These coverlets became very popular just before a panoply of blue and white quilt designs emerged.

ECB Feathered Stars Quilt

* Quiltmaker unidentified, pieced initials ECB, possibly New York State; 1850–60
* Cotton
* height 95½ width 76½"
* Collection of the American Folk Art Museum, New York
* Gift of Cyril Irwin Nelson
  1985.36.1 Photo by Matt Hoebermann

HEARTS AND PINEAPPLES QUILT TOP

This quilt, probably from Pennsylvania, dates from 1850 to 1870. The main part of the quilt is divided into six square symmetrical blocks joined by thin strips of sashing. The usual way of making patterns for such appliqué was by cutting out folded paper squares, thereby achieving symmetrical patterns. These central blocks have a strong clean-lined design based on hearts and pineapples. Three sides of the quilt have a border, a regularly waving stem from where groups of three leaves sprout. Rather than bearing flowers or fruit, pairs of birds perch on the stem, sharing between them a berry. With such symbols it is possible that this was a betrothal or marriage quilt.

Hearts and Pineapples Quilt Top

* Quiltmaker unidentified, probably Pennsylvania; c. 1850–70
* Cotton
* height 87" width 69½"
* Collection of the American Folk Art Museum, New York
* Gift of Cyril Irwin Nelson in memory of his grandparents, Guerdon Stearns and Elinor Irwin (Chase) Holden, and in honor of his parents, Cyril Arthur and Elise Macy Nelson
  1982.22.4

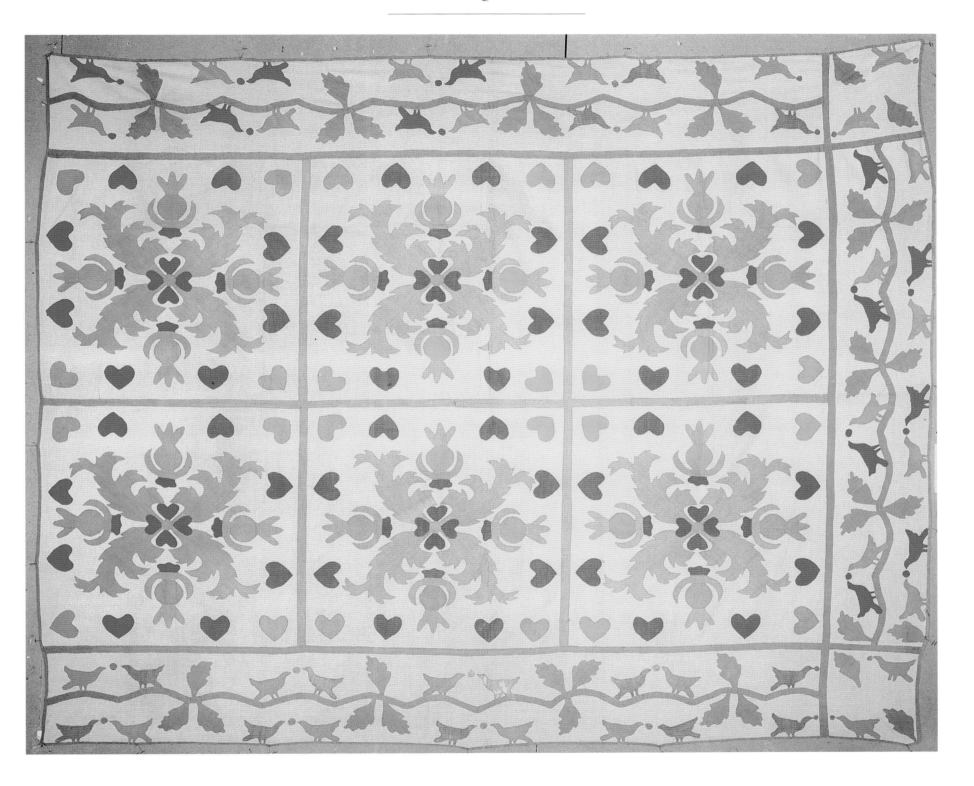

FLORAL MEDALLION QUILT

While this cotton appliqué quilt, dating from 1870 to 1880 can definitely be classified as a medallion quilt, the central motif has become so large that it almost completely fills the quilt top and has transformed into more of a frame than a medallion. This triple-ringed frame made of yellow, pink and green provides stability for the tulips, waterlilies, daisies, and oak leaves that sprout from it towards the edges of the quilt. A slim undulating vine, sporting a reduced selection of flora, meanders around the edge of the quilt that is finally bound with a narrow green strip. Apart from a single feather in each corner, the quilting is kept to a restrained equidistant criss-cross of straight lines. The result is a striking well-balanced, tasteful quilt.

Floral Medallion Quilt

* Quiltmaker unidentified, possibly Vincennes, Indiana; 1870–80
* Cotton
* height 86" width 70"
* Collection of the American Folk Art Museum, New York
* Gift of Irene Reichert
  1993.1.3 Photo by Matt Hoebermann

OAK LEAF WITH CHERRIES QUILT

This bold symmetrical quilt, almost square, is somewhat unusual in that it has no border. Instead, each corner contains a cherry and leaf motif. Apart from a few small accents of chrome yellow, the colors used are the popular white, red, and green. This is not merely due to aesthetic reasons or fashion, but to cost, availability, and technicalities. The use of plain undyed cotton for the largest expanse of fabric kept the cost down, and at a time when many dyes were unstable, the familiar turkey red, though expensive, was a reliable choice for a quilt intended to last, as it was one of the more permanent dyes. Though greens of the period were prone to fading to a green with a yellow or blue tinge, they still provided an effective contrast to the bright turkey red. The quilt dates from 1870 to 1880 and is made completely from cotton apart from the stems of the cherries and the tulips which are embroidered in stem stitch with wool.

Oak Leaf with Cherries Quilt

* Quiltmaker unidentified, United States; 1870–80
* Cotton with wool embroidery
* height 80" width 78"
* Collection of the American Folk Art Museum, New York
* Gift of Irene Reichert
  1993.1.1 Photo by Matt Hoebermann

LOG CABIN QUILT, COURTHOUSE STEPS VARIATION

This all-cotton quilt top has no backing, thereby revealing the foundation fabric blocks onto which the "logs" were sewn. This top is made in the "Courthouse Steps" variation of log cabin, in which the darks are arranged squarely opposite the darks and the lights squarely opposite the lights. It is then essential to arrange this block so that the darks join with another block made from the same fabric. This top is somewhat unusual in that each block is only constructed from two different fabrics rather than a selection. Half the fabrics used in this top are madder-dyed browns, the remainder of the quilt, including the border, are constructed of a solid white cloth. In common with the majority of log cabin quilts, this top is tied rather than quilted.

Log Cabin Quilt,
Courthouse Steps Variation

* Quiltmaker unidentified, United States, 1870–90
* Cotton
* height 81¼" width 79¾"
* Collection of the American Folk Art Museum, New York
* Gift of Mrs. Alice Kaplan
  1977.13.6 Photo by Matt Hoebermann

CENTER STAR CRAZY THROW

Crazy quilts were made as show pieces and this one was probably intended as a parlor throw. It was designed by the quilter—Mary Ann Crocker Hinman—herself and features a central star surrounded by fans—one of the most popular Japanese inspired motifs. This is not a true "crazy" as its execution is not random, but it is a crazy in spirit with its use of luxurious fabrics and wonderful working of color. Crazy quilts became hugely popular following the 1876 Philadephia Centennial Exhibition when Japanese objects and style were appreciated for the first time in the United States.

Center Star Crazy Throw

* Mary Ann Crocker Hinman (1817–93),
  New York State; 1880-1890
* Silk with silk embroidery
* h.64 w.52¾"
* Collection of the American Folk Art Museum,
  New York
* Gift of Ruth E. Avard
* 1993.2.1 Photo by Matt Hoebermann

MAP QUILT

Dated 1886 in embroidered Roman numerals, this crazy quilt is of silk and cotton with silk embroidery. The main elements of this quilt are the background of pieced "Y" shapes and the central part in which the crazy element of the quilt depicts the map of the United States. Each piece of the map is a different state, five of which have the addition of an embroidered symbol: a star in Texas; flowers in Illinois, Iowa, and Wyoming; and a spider's web in Colorado. It is not clear whether these states have any particular significance to the maker or if the quilt perhaps remained unfinished.

Map Quilt

* Quiltmaker unidentified, possibly Virginia; 1886
* Silk velvets and brocades with silk embroidery
* height 78¾" width 82¼"
* Collection of the American Folk Art Museum, New York
* Gift of Dr. and Mrs. C. David McLaughlin 1987.1.1 Photo by Schecter Lee

BOXER DOG CRAZY MAT

This "Boxer Dog Crazy Mat" from the collection of the American Folk Art Museum is made of silk with a lace edging and silk and wool embroidery. The piece is thought to date from 1885 to 1895 and has the initials "JJJ" elaborately embroidered in the bottom right-hand corner. The small size of this piece—under three-feet square—has made it possible for it to be pieced onto one single foundation piece of cloth rather than onto a series of smaller pieces of cloth. This quilt is completely crazy: there does not appear to be any overall plan regarding the positioning of color or sizes of pieces. Even the placing of the dog appears to be unplanned. The seams between pieces are decorated with embroidery, as are many of the darker pieces of fabric, and the mat is finished off with a slim binding and a lace edging.

Boxer Dog Crazy Mat

*   Probably Mrs. Triece, initialed JJJ, Pennsylvania; 1885–95
*   Silks, with lace edging, and silk and wool embroidery
*   height 37" width 30" with lace trimming
*   Collection of the American Folk Art Museum, New York
*   Gift of Margaret Cavigga 1985.23.5

PRINCESS FEATHER QUILT

The women of the Walker household in the vicinity of Oak Ridge, Missouri have resisted any over-complication with this cotton quilt made between 1880 and 1900. The quilt has been designed with great restraint. The central part is divided into four squares. Radiating from each centrally placed, two-tone, eight-pointed star are eight "princess feathers" appliquéd in two different tones. Rather than load the quilt with a heavy pieced border, the Walker women have chosen to appliqué four pairs of two-tone leaves along each edge of the quilt top. Finally the quilt has been finished off with narrow binding. Inspection of the binding of a quilt can often help with deducing a date of manufacture. If the binding has been cut on the bias, then the quilt probably dates from the twentieth century: in the previous century binding was usually cut along the straight grain of the fabric.

Princess Feather Quilt

* Women of the Walker household, vicinity of Oak Ridge, Missouri; 1880–1900
* Cotton
* height 83" width 81"
* Collection of the American Folk Art Museum, New York
* Gift of Beverly Walker Reitz in memory of Vest Walker 1984.22.2 Photo by Matt Hoebermann

LOG CABIN QUILT, PINEAPPLE VARIATION

This variation on the log cabin design was probably made in Lancaster County, Pennsylvania between 1880 and 1890. This variation is more difficult to make than either the barn-raising or courthouse steps versions. The ends of the "logs" are cut across at an angle to give a saw-tooth effect that suggests either a pineapple or the action of windmill blades in motion: as a consequence of the jagged ends, the pieces are more difficult to assemble. The striking color combination of bright red and yellow succeeds in disguising the outlines of the blocks from which the top is assembled. The color scheme is maintained in the border of pieced diagonal strips and the simple narrow red binding.

Log Cabin Quilt, Pineapple Variation

* Quiltmaker unidentified, possibly Lancaster County, Pennsylvania; 1880-1900
* Cotton
* height 83¼" width 83"
* Collection of the American Folk Art Museum, New York
* Gift of Kinuko Fujii, Osaka, Japan
  1991.8.1 Photo by Scott Bowron

LOG CABIN QUILT, WINDMILL BLADES VARIATION

This variation of a log cabin quilt was made in silk by Ada Hapman (Mrs. William) Kingsley of South Windsor, New York, or Athens, Pennsylvania in the last twenty years of the nineteenth century. The granddaughter of the maker reported that the quilt was never used as it was the only one that her grandmother made out of silk. Unlike the pineapple version shown on page 73, the blocks that make up the design are clearly visible. A wide variety of fabrics, both dark and light, have been gathered and saved to create this elaborate variation of a log cabin quilt. Though the planning of the quilt itself is complex, the maker has gone further by completing her work with a border pieced from triangles constructed of strips in both a range of colored fabrics and black, finally adding a scalloped border of black.

Log Cabin Quilt, Windmill Blades Variation

* Ada Hapman (Mrs. William) Kingsley (1859-1939), South Windsor, New York, or Athens, Pennsylvania; 1880-1900
* Silk
* height 73" width 65"
* Collection of the American Folk Art Museum, New York
* Gift of Margaret Cavigga 1985.23.6 Photo by Matt Hoebermann

S. H. CRAZY QUILT

Initialed "S.H" and dating from 1885 to 1895 this quilt is on a foundation of silk, ink, paint, and cotton silk embroidery. The main part of the quilt is divided into forty-nine squares, each pieced and embroidered and then sewn together to make the quilt top which is completed with two quilted plain borders and a final slim binding. The quilt writers Kiracofe and Johnson suggest that the Centennial Exposition in Philadelphia triggered the adoption of various decorative art innovations that emanated from Japan. This together with exposure to the aesthetic movement, promoted by the lecture tours of Oscar Wilde and the decreasing price of silk to home production emerged as an outpouring of flamboyant, asymmetrically arranged, richly colored crazy quilts. Mixed with this exoticism in this quilt are blocks featuring figures of children, which may well have been taken from a book of outline embroidery designs published by Kate Greenaway.

S. H. Crazy Quilt

* Quiltmaker unidentifed, initialed S.H.,
  United States; 1885–95
* Silk, ink, paint, and cotton with silk embroidery
* height 75" width 74"
* Collection of the American Folk Art Museum,
  New York
* Gift of Margaret Cavigga
  985.23.4 Photo by Matt Hoebermann

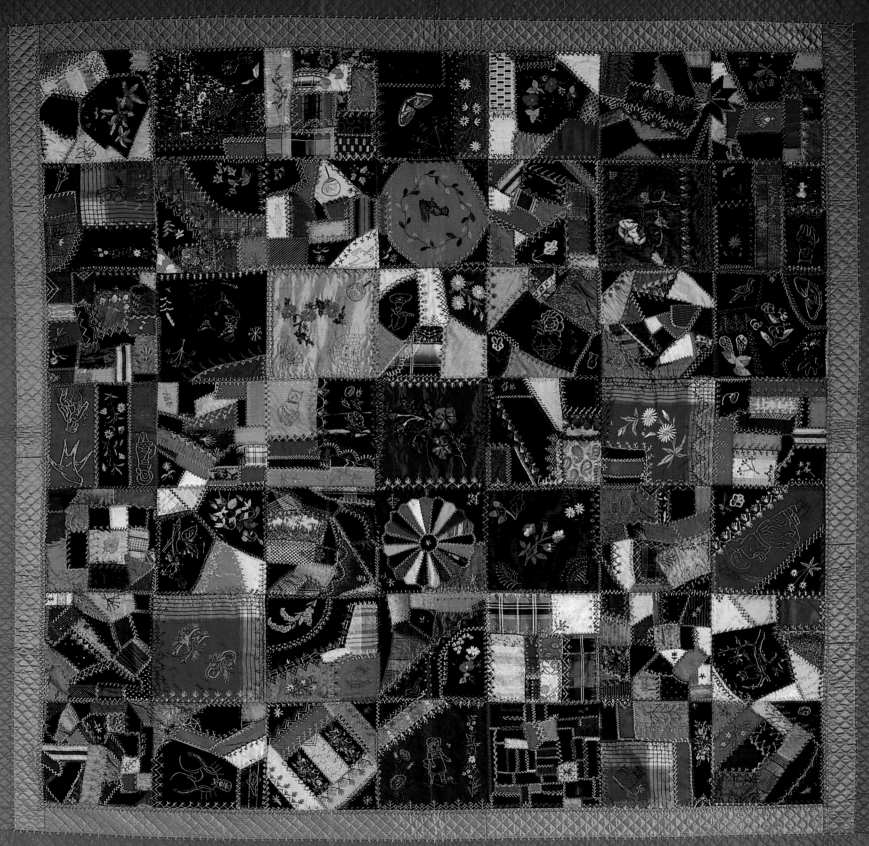

LOG CABIN QUILT, BARN-RAISING VARIATION

Another quilt from Mifflin County, Pennsylvania, this time a wool and cotton log cabin quilt made between 1890 and 1900 by Lydia A. (Kanagy) Peachey, a member of the Yellow Topper Amish. Lydia Peachey was well behind fashion in the outside world, as this wool and cotton log cabin quilt was often made by quiltmakers in the 1860s. By the turn of the century, it had become the fashion to make such quilts out of fabrics such as silk and keep them merely for show. At first glance it would appear that Lydia Peachey had constructed the quilt entirely from plain solid color fabric. However, a second look reveals that some of the "chimneys" or center squares of the blocks are cut out of printed fabrics.

Log Cabin Quilt, Barn-Raising Variation

* Lydia A. (Kanagy) Peachey, Yellow Topper Amish (1863-1949), Mifflin County, Pennsylvania; 1890-1900
* Wool and cotton
* height 85" width 80½"
* Collection of the American Folk Art Museum, New York
* Gift of Mr. and Mrs. William B. Wigton 1984.25.14 Photo by Schecter Lee

DOUBLE WEDDING RING CANDLEWICK SPREAD

Another example of whitework, this quilt by an unidentified quilt maker dates from June 1897. This all-over patterned quilt is a fine example of the technique known as candlewicking or roving. This quilt ably demonstrates how once a pattern enters into the vocabulary of a craft, it has the ability to be adapted to a variety of techniques. "Double wedding ring" is a pattern that is a favorite with experienced piecework quilters. In piecework or patchwork, small segments of rings are sewn together to make a series of interlocking rings that cover the quilt top. The pattern is a symbol of matrimonial happiness, and while it is more usual to see it executed in patchwork, here it has been candlewicked onto a white ground.

Double Wedding Ring
Candlewick Spread

* Maker unidentified, United States; June 1897
* Cotton with clipped cotton roving
* height 79¾" width 65"
* Collection of the American Folk Art Museum, New York
* Gift of Robert Bishop
  1990.25.1

SCHOOLHOUSE QUILT TOP

The use of just two plain fabrics and only one block throughout allows the orderly arrangement of the numerous names on this signature quilt to become an integral part of the design. The quilt was made 1897–98 in cotton with cotton embroidery by "The Presbyterian Ladies of Oak Ridge, Missouri." The effectiveness of the pattern is the repetition of a single block. Each schoolhouse is a pieced block set into the quilt top with white background strips. "Schoolhouse" was a popular pattern in the second half of the nineteenth century and ideally suited to being made by a group of people. This and similar patterns achieved a second wave of popularity with the quilting revival in the second decade of the twentieth century. Similar patterns had different names. Ruby McKim's book *101 Patchwork Patterns*, originally published in 1931, details "House on the Hill," which bears a striking resemblance to "Schoolhouse;" however, she suggests using several patterned fabrics for the areas around the house to suggest a hill and a garden. Her design for "Honeymoon Cottage" is a more involved design, perhaps requiring more accurate piecing.

Schoolhouse Quilt Top

* The Presbyterian Ladies of Oak Ridge, Missouri; 1897–98
* Cotton with cotton embroidery
* height 74½" w. 90½"
* Collection of the American Folk Art Museum, New York
* Gift of Beverly Walker Reitz in memory of Vest Walker 1984.22.10 Photo by Matt Hoebermann

MISSOURI BRIDAL CRAZY QUILT

This quilt of wool and cotton with wool embroidery is dated 1900 and was made by May Dodge Harper of Poplar Bluff, Missouri. Unlike the "Boxer Dog Crazy Mat," this quilt top is made of eighteen or more blocks which have been constructed separately and sewn together later. This division into blocks, the joining seams of which have been embroidered over, lends a certain regularity to the overall design. Certain motifs and symbols sewn onto the quilt also confirm suggestions that this is a bridal quilt: two conjoined hearts take a prominent position in one of the central blocks, while a horseshoe lies in one of the upper blocks.

Missouri Bridal Crazy Quilt

* May Dodge Harper, Poplar Bluff, Missouri; 1900
* Wool and cotton with wool embroidery
* height 91½" width 66¼"
* Collection of the American Folk Art Museum, New York
* Gift of Margaret Cavigga
  1985.23.1

ADMIRAL DEWEY COMMEMORATIVE QUILT

This signature quilt was made at the turn of the twentieth century. The quilt is made of cotton with turkey red cotton embroidery. By the middle of the nineteenth century it was commonplace for funds to be raised for charitable purposes by the making of quilts. Contributors would make a specified donation, often a dime, to have their name either written or embroidered onto the quilt which was either raffled to raise further funds or given to a local dignitary. Often the size of donation dictated the prominence of the signature. The embroidery in the center of this quilt reads "Admiral Dewey Commander of United States Navy." From the 1890s to the 1920s patterns were published for Dewey quilts, and it is likely that the idea of embroidering names in the shape of a letter "D" came from such a source. Dewey served in the Union Navy during the Civil War but is best known for his defeat of the enemy fleet during the Spanish-American War of 1898, for which it is possible that this quilt was used to raise money.

Admiral Dewey Commemorative Quilt

* Possibly the Mite Society (Ladies' Aid), United Brethren Church, Center-Point, Indiana; 1900–10
* Cotton with Turkey red cotton embroidery
* height 88" width 65"
* Collection of the American Folk Art Museum, New York
* Gift of Janet Gilbert for Marie Griffin 1993.3.1 Photo by Matt Hoebermann

DIAMOND IN THE SQUARE QUILT

This quilt was made in 1903 by Rebecca Fisher Stolzfus in the Groffdale area of Lancaster County, Pennsylvania. It is made of wool with a rayon binding that was added later. The pattern only occurs in Lancaster County and was adapted from quilts of the nineteenth century in which the quilt was based around a central medallion. Amish quilts have much in common with the whole-cloth quilts of the late-eighteenth and early-nineteenth century. This example demonstrates the use of large expanses of one piece of material. Where it differs from the whole-cloth quilts is in the use of contrasting colors to emphasize the change from one piece to another. It has been suggested that this common design with four corner pieces developed from the embossed decorations on Amish hymnals.

Diamond in the Square Quilt

* Rebecca Fisher Stoltzfus, Groffdale area of Lancaster County, Pennsylvania; 1903
* Wool; rayon binding added later
* height 77" width 77"
* Collection of the American Folk Art Museum, New York
* Gift of Mr. and Mrs. William B. Wigton 1984.25.1 Photo by Schecter Lee

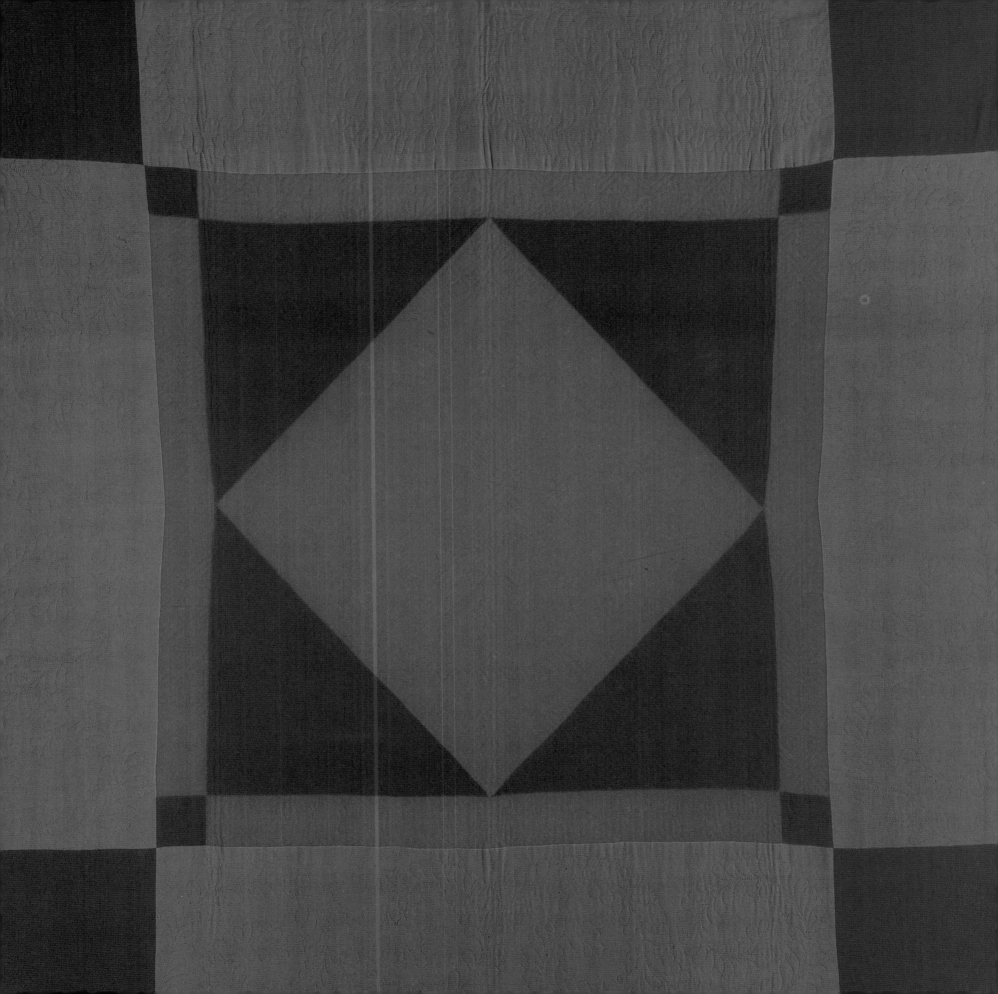

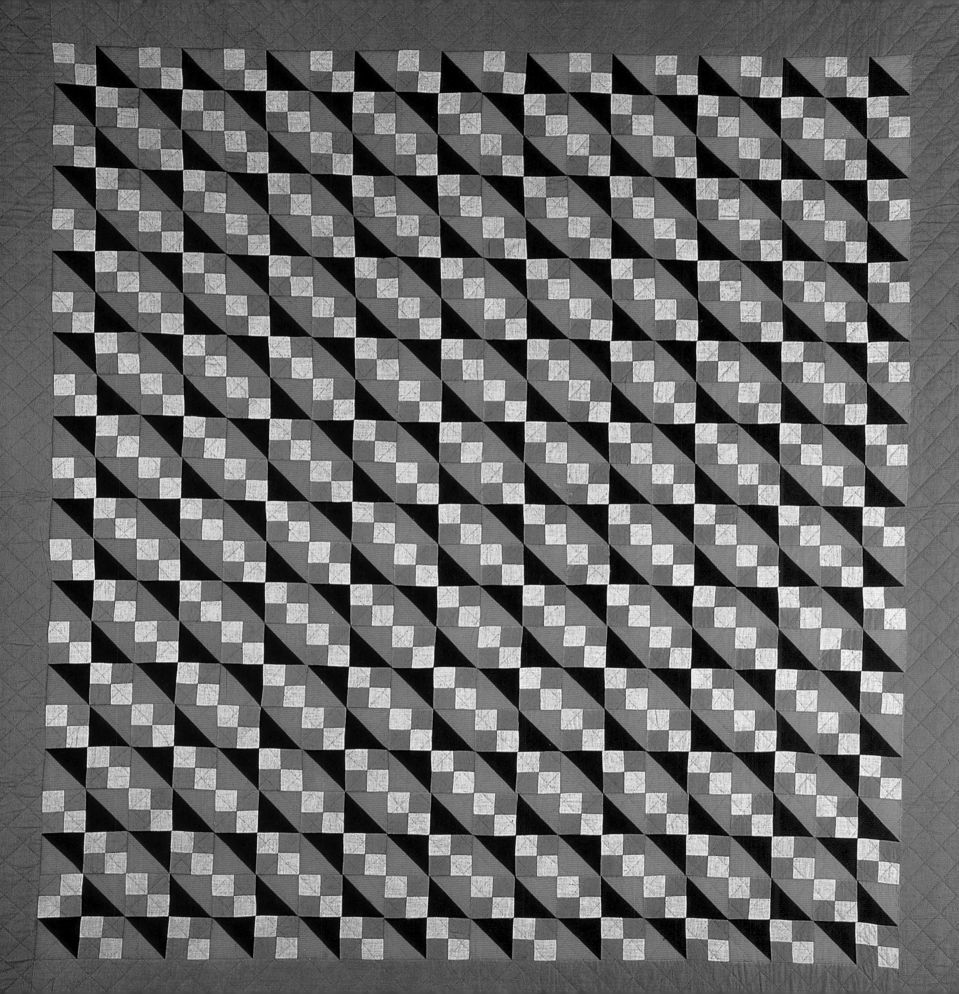

FOUR PATCH
IN TRIANGLES QUILT

Amish groups have lived in Mifflin County, Pennsylvania since the 1790s when several families moved from Lancaster County. This quilt was made by Barbara Zook Peachey (1848–1930), a member of the Byler Church, or Yellow Topper Amish, for her granddaughter, Katie M. Peachey. The use of four- and nine-patch quilts was common among the stricter Amish groups. Indeed, in some church groups these were the only patterns permitted. The repetition of this overall pattern in the main part of the quilt is relieved by several changes of color. The center column of blocks is executed in blue and black, placed next to columns of red and black. The placing of these different colored blocks is symmetrical apart from a brown and black block in the top left corner where one would expect to see red: whether this is intentional or not is unclear.

Four Patch in Triangles Quilt

* Barbara Zook Peachey, Yellow Topper Amish, Mifflin County, Pennsylvania; 1910–20
* Cotton, sateen
* height 85½" width 78¾"
* Collection of the American Folk Art Museum, New York
* Gift of Mr. and Mrs. William B. Wigton 1984.25.12 Photo by Schecter Lee

FOUR IN SPLIT NINE-PATCH QUILT

Each of the five groups in Mifflin County, Pennsylvania can be distinguished from the others. Each group has rules that cover the style and color of clothing worn. Their horse-drawn buggies are of different styles, easily differentiated by the color on the top of the buggy roof; their styles of housing and decoration are different and this extends to the quilts that they make. This cotton quilt with cotton embroidery was made between 1920 and 1930 by Lydia A. (Yoder) Hostetler, a member of the White Topper Amish. The quilt is embroidered "LAY". The central part of the quilt is made up in blocks of four in split nine patches which is then surrounded by two quilted borders, the quilting of one resembling rainbow shapes.

Four in Split Nine-Patch Quilt

* Lydia A. (Yoder) Hostetler, White Topper Amish,
  Mifflin County Pennsylvania; 1920–30
* Cotton with cotton embroidery
* height 77" width 67"
* Collection of the American Folk Art Museum,
  New York
* Gift of Mr. and Mrs. William B. Wigton
  1984.25.7 Photo by Schecter Lee

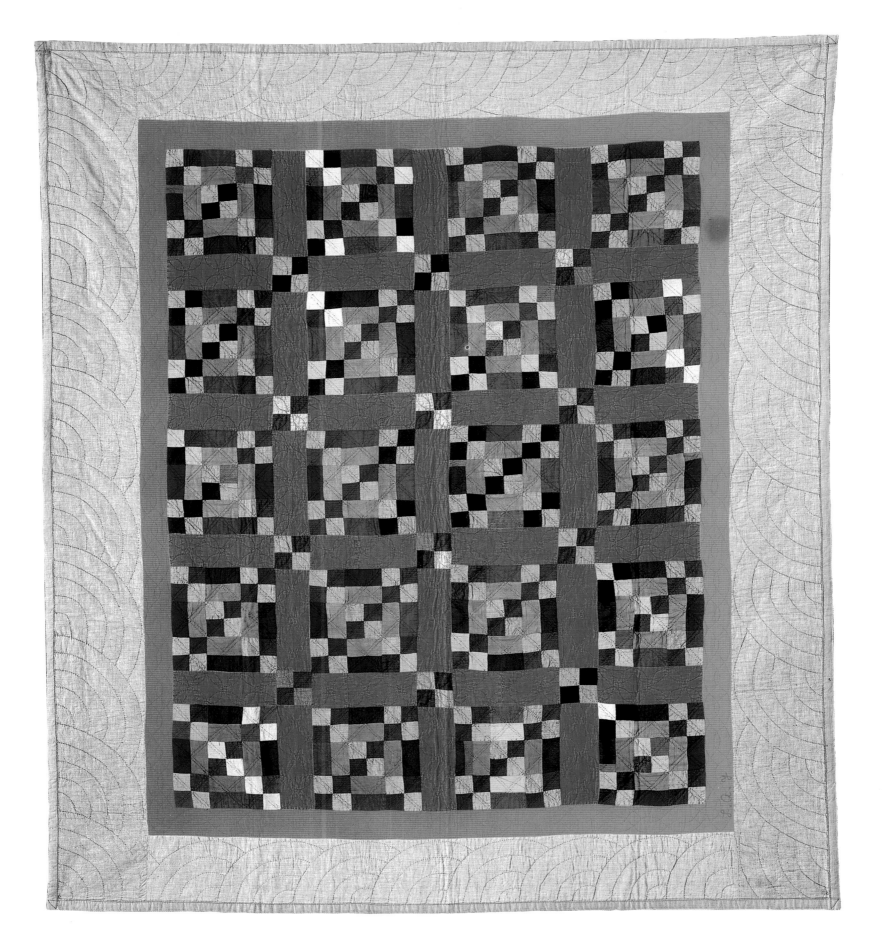

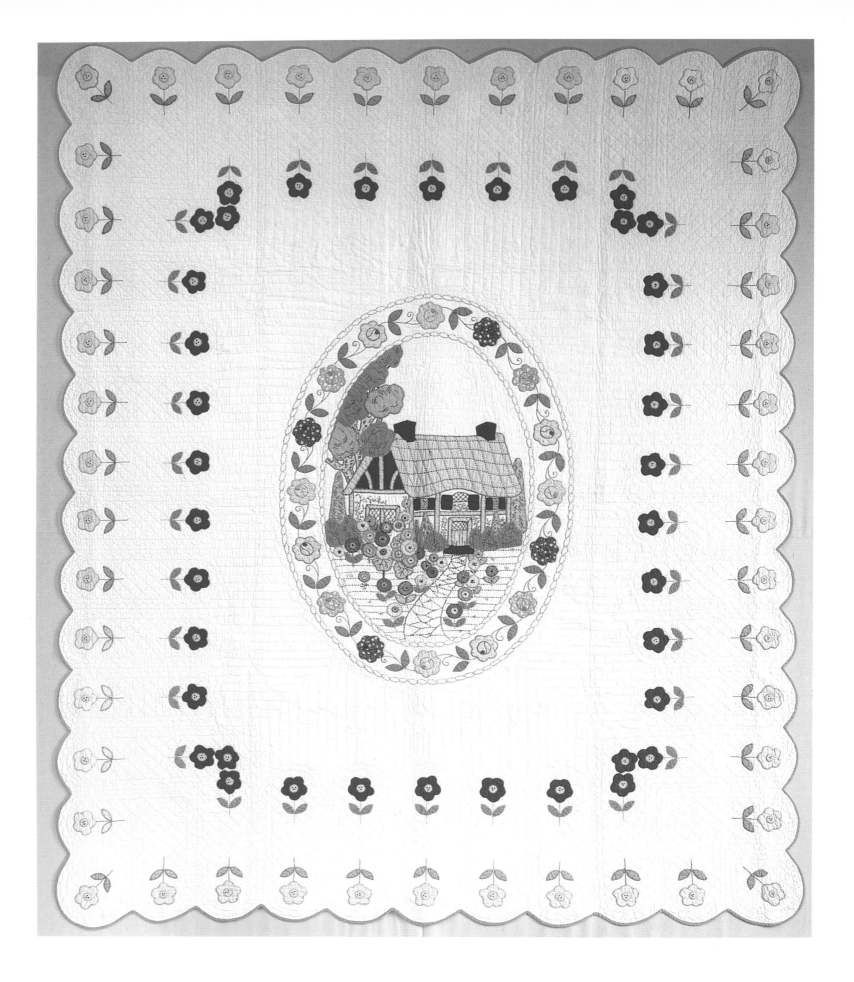

HOLLYHOCK COTTAGE QUILT

This rectangular twentieth century quilt dates from the immediate pre-World War II period. Made in cotton with cotton embroidery, in common with the previous quilt, the design is based around a central medallion. Very much of its period, this central element of the quilt is typical of the themes and design elements predominant in textiles and ceramics of this time, though the floral border of the medallion could be said to show the influences of both Germanic patterns and Jacobean textile designs. This appliquéd medallion is enhanced with embroidery in cotton. Great use is made of the white void between medallion and borders to avoid the quilt top becoming overcrowded. The two borders of simple, single flowers are framed by a scalloped, colored binding.

Hollyhock Cottage Quilt

* Quiltmaker unidentified, United States; 1930–40
* Cotton with cotton embroidery
* height 88¼" width 72½"
* Collection of the American Folk Art Museum, New York
* Gift of Margaret Cavigga
  1988.28.2 Photo by Matt Hoebermann

ALL AMERICAN STAR QUILT

Dating from the World War II period this cotton quilt is probably from New York State. Though the dyes used would not be the indigo and turkey red so popular a hundred years earlier, the color contrast of red with white and blue with white has been maximized by combining all three in a cleverly arranged top that patriotically displays thirty blue stars within thirty red stars. The choice of both plain solid and polka-dotted fabrics results in a design that appears almost three-dimensional. The white areas of the quilt have been quilted in a diamond or kite-shape pattern, thereby retaining the obtuse angles produced by the points of the stars. The lack of a contrasting binding serves to retain the three-dimensionality of the design.

All American Star Quilt

* Quiltmaker unidentified, New York State; 1940–45
* Cotton
* height 87" width 72"
* Collection of the American Folk Art Museum, New York
* Gift of Cyril Irwin Nelson 1987.17.2

QUILT MUSEUM IN KENTUCKY

These two quilts hanging in a quilt museum in Kentucky demonstrate how the idea of a show quilt has persisted until the end of the twentieth century. Quilting has almost permanently lost its image as a pragmatic art and been transformed into a craft for those with time on their hands or an artistic inclination. There can no doubt that the fabrics used were bought specifically for the manufacture of these quilts and that the quilts were never intended as bedcoverings. Both quilts have a central medallion as a starting point for their design. The pink quilt on the right then relies on a graded change of color in the borders to enhance the basket applique in the central medallion. The other quilt works in a reverse way to the first quilt. The central medallion in this quilt is fairly small and the design simple, it is the border which contains the complicated piecing.

Quilts in Museum

* Various
* Various
* Unknown
* Collection of the Kentucky Quilt Museum,
* © Raymond Gehman/CORBIS

THE AIDS MEMORIAL QUILT

The AIDS Memorial Quilt is the largest quilt ever made. Begun in June 1987 the purpose of the quilt is fourfold: to remember who have died of AIDS; to heal those who have lost someone to AIDS; to promote awareness of AIDS; and to educate by revealing the truth about AIDS and how to prevent further deaths. The AIDS Memorial Quilt is the largest community art project ever undertaken: there are now more than 44,000 panels in existence, each one measuring six feet by three feet and in memory of an individual who has died of AIDS. On October 11, 1987, during the National March on Washington for Lesbian and Gay Rights, the quilt was put on display for the first time, on the National Mall in Washington, D.C. Half a million people visited the display of 1,920 panels. The quilt went on tour for four months to twenty cities raising $500,000 for AIDS organizations. As the tour progressed, panels were added till the number increased to six thousand, finally returning at the end of two years to have grown to eight thousand two hundred and eighty-eight. In 1989, the quilt was nominated for the Nobel Peace Prize.

The AIDS Memorial Quilt

* Various; since June 1987
* Various
* Constantly increasing
* © Lee Snider; Lee Snider/CORBIS

SPACIOUS SKIES QUILT

This quilt by Charlotte Warr-Andersen of Kearns, Utah was the second prize winner in The Great American Quilt Contest in Celebration of the Statue of Liberty Centennial in 1986. The quilt is made of cotton and polyester blends. In common with a great many contemporary quilts, this item was never intended to be used as a bedcovering and belongs to what is now known as "fiber art." Entries to the competition had to adhere strictly to the rules. Quilts were to be full size, measuring 72 inches x 72 inches with two inches tolerance, and were marked on design, execution, and interpretation of the design brief. The quilt combines the use of pictorial elements with traditional pieced and quilted designs. The Statue of Liberty, two other landmarks in the upper part of the quilt, and two events of significance to twentieth century Americans in the lower half of the quilt are enclosed by pieced and quilted borders. All these areas of this piece of fiber art are firmly delineated by the use of wide white sashing.

Spacious Skies Quilt

* Charlotte Warr-Anderson, Kearns, Utah; 1985–86
* Cotton and polyester
* height 72" width 71½"
* Collection of the American Folk Art Museum, New York
* The Scotchgard ® Collection of Contemporary Quilts, Second Prize Winner, the Great American Quilt Contest, in celebration of the Statue of Liberty Centennial, 1986
  1986.14.2

CHILDHOOD MEMORY #44 THE CELLAR:

"DON'T WORRY," SAID HIS SISTER SWEETLY, "I WON'T TURN OFF THE LIGHT..."

Elaine H. Spencer of Fort Collins, Colorado achieved First Place Grand Prize Winner in the 1988 "Memories of Childhood" contest, which was part of Great American Quilt Festival 2, an event arranged by the American Folk Art Museum. In this second contest, competitors were asked to make a crib quilt on the theme of "Memories of Childhood." Elaine Spencer chose to depict a genuine incident from her childhood. In common with the majority of those who entered the competition, Spencer chose to make a representational quilt, using carefully chosen fabrics and overdying in place of artist's paints. The quilted borders serve to support this treatment of the quilt as a painting.

Childhood Memory #44 The Cellar:

"Don't worry," said his sister sweetly, "I won't turn off the light . . ."

* Elaine H. Spencer, Fort Collins, Colorado; 1988
* Cotton
* height 51¼" width 43"
* Collection of the American Folk Art Museum, New York
* First Place Grand Prize Winner "Memories of Childhood" Contest, The Great American Quilt Festival 2, museum event sponsored by Fairfield Processing Corporation/Poly-fil ®. Springmaid ® and Coats & Clark, Inc./Dual Duty Plus ® Quilting.
* 1989.23.1 Photo by Scott Bowron

QUILTING IN POIPU, HAWAII

This woman shown quilting in Poipu, Hawaii in 1991 demonstrates how the traditions and designs of one culture have cross-fertilized with those of others. The first white women, most of them wives of missionaries, arrived in Hawaii in 1820 and in the following years the native women were taught New England-style piece or patchwork. Mission schools also taught paper-cutting or *Scherenschnitte* and it would appear that these skills merged with Hawaiian traditions of making bedcoverings from thin sheets of white mulberry tree bark. This has resulted in the instantly recognizable Hawaiian quilting style of the last century and a quarter. Rather than creating a quilt top of many blocks, the Hawaiian quilt is either an all-over design or confined to a few large blocks. The primary part of the design is a symmetrical appliquéd piece, usually in red or some other bright color. What causes a Hawaiian quilt to stand out as being from Hawaii is the manner in which the quilting stitches are executed. Hawaiian quilts make extensive use of echo quilting. The lines and outlines of the appliquéd pieces are "echoed" with lines of quilting that follow both the internal and external lines of the pieces.

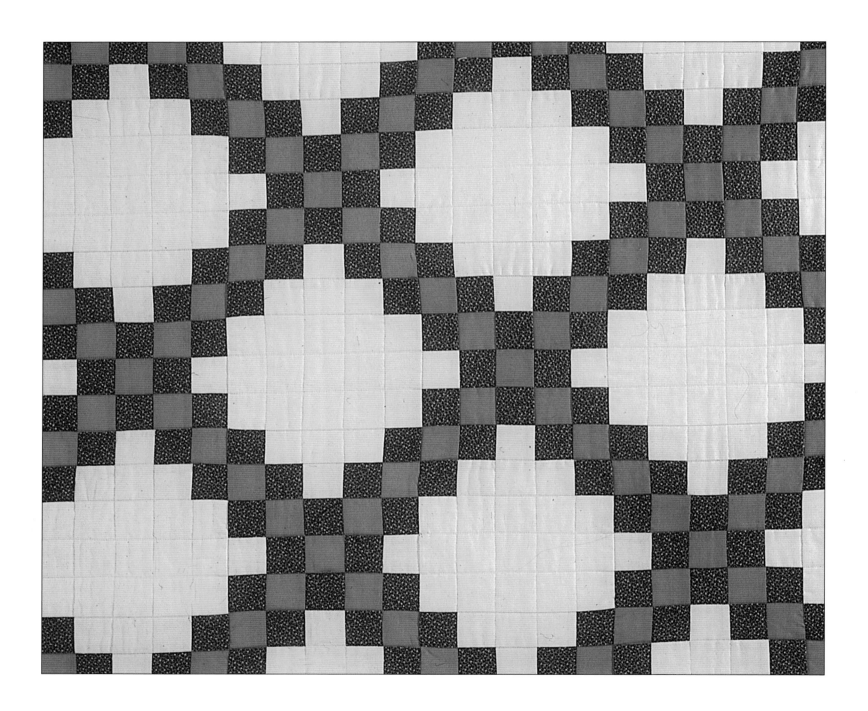

IRISH CHAIN QUILT

What we know as the Irish Chain is called the American Chain in Ireland. Actually, there is no hard and fast evidence of where the style originated. It is certainly a traditional patchwork design—variations have been seen for centuries—but it is difficult to identify the original tradition! The variation shown here is Double Irish Chain, the most popular of the numerous variations.

      The Irish Chain is not at all difficult to make and is a perfect starting point for the beginner. In spite of its seeming complexity, in fact the design is made up of of two basic blocks that are pieced individually. The Double Irish Chain is made of chains, pieced by machine, that are three small squares wide, made in two strongly contrasting colors—here gray and orange—against a solid off-white background. The solid areas provide scope for simple or elaborate quilting, depending on the level of expertise of the quilter.

Strips of fabric are machined together along their length and then cut
across to form the patterns for this quilt.

AMISH BARS QUILT

A straightforward Amish design, this is another quilt that is perfect for the beginner. The cutting can be managed quickly with a rotary cutter, and the piecing simply requires the stitching of a few straight seams. The only difficult thing is getting the right color combination—with such a simple design, the colors and texture of the fabric double in importance.

 While the example illustrated was made from wool crepe, if you choose to make the quilt in plain cottons, finish it with simple quilting. The traditional Amish quilting design used for quilts like this is crosshatching, something that can be done quickly on a machine.

This quilt is made from strips joined at their long edges, bordered, and backed. If done in cotton, quilting is easily accomplished.

LOG CABIN QUILT

There are many ways to make a log cabin quilt—from cutting strips and chain-piecing them to making multiple blocks. Log cabin quilts can be sewn by hand, by adding strips individually around a center square, or by applying the square and then the strips to a backing square of cloth. Miniature log cabin quilts can be fashioned on a tiny scale by using narrow strips and a backing of interlining printed with a grid pattern.

This log cabin quilt was made using a method that saw each block pieced and stitched to a heavy batting at the same time. An extremely quick way to quilt, it has its dangers for the inexperienced, but it is a good way to do log cabin quilting, as it is a straightfoward design. Even the borders can be worked in this quick method before adding batting and backing.

Log cabin quilts are not suitable for elaborate quilting—they just have too many seams, and most other methods of producing them involve more layers than are found in many other quilts.

After cutting the strips for the blocks, attach them to squares of cotton and batting. These are then stitched in rows and finished with a suitable border.

PINWHEEL QUILT

Quilts like this have been made for centuries in India and Pakistan, and many of the earliest designs use simple geometric patterns like this pinwheel. The most striking feature of these designs is their bold coloring, which was laden with symbolism—for example, the saffron yellow used here recalls the earth, and red is the color of love.

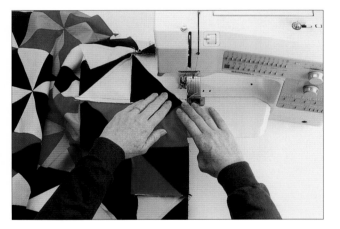

Cut pairs of squares from contrasting colors, combining the pieced triangle blocks to make four-patch blocks that can be placed into the overall design effectively. Border and—if desired—tassel.

AMISH STAR BABY QUILT

Another Amish design, this baby quilt is typical of Amish quilting—in particular the center square with its borders that alternate between light and dark colors.

      The central medallion is a variation of a traditional star pattern called Evening Star. The eight-point star appears in many different guises in the center of Amish quilts—as the Star of Bethlehem, made from diamond-shaped scraps, and the Ohio Star, which looks like Evening Star but is made from a nine-patch block. Note that the border sees not only the difference between dark and light colors but also a difference in thickness. Too thick and the dark bands will overpower the light. Note, too, the strips inserted above and below the sawtooth border to lengthen the quilt and make it rectangular.

      The quilt has some simple machine quilting; there is scope for much more hand quilting—particularly along the unpieced borders.

 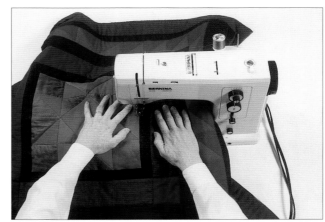

Pieced and plain squares alternate in this vibrant patchwork design.

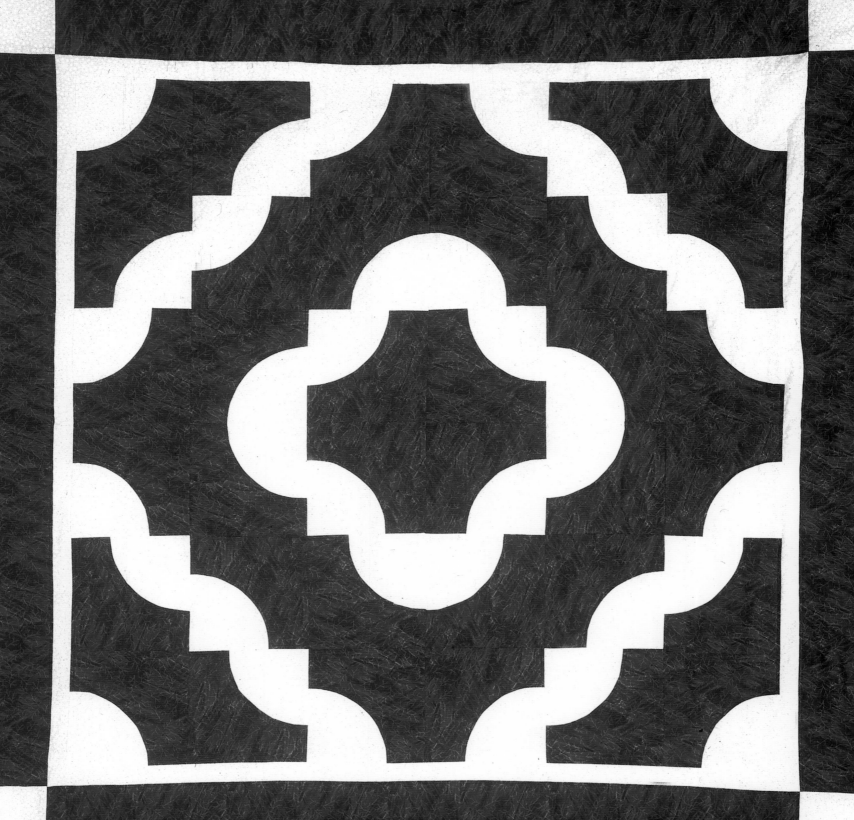

CHAIN LINKS QUILT

This is a variation of the drunkard's path pattern discussed on page 14. It uses the same two shapes to make squares, which can be arranged to create a ring.

Drunkard's path has many variations—such as Wonder of the World, Falling Timbers, Dove, Love Ring, Snowball, and Fool's Puzzle. All are based on a square with a curved "bite" taken out of one corner. Any of the drunkard's path designs can be made as scrap quilts, but choice of fabric color is important or you will lose the pattern.

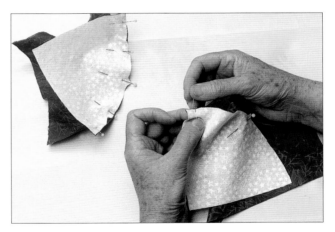

Careful use of two templates allows the two-colored blocks to be configured in rows to give the pattern.

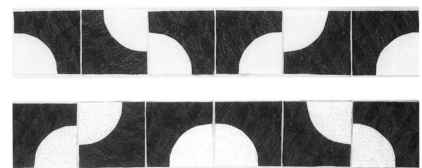

CENTER DIAMOND QUILT

The last of the three Amish designs illustrated in this section, the Center Diamond quilt is typical of Amish patchwork design, combining simplicity, style, and traditional values. As with so much Amish design, the simplicity hides the complexity of construction. Here, the difficulty is in the long bias-cut seams, which must be sewn very carefully to stop them from stretching—although you can hide any distortion by heavy quilting. Indeed, the beauty of this design is that it does afford the quilter a chance to quilt.

The Center Diamond pattern—also known as Diamond in the Square—has many variations. The diamond can be a plain piece of cloth, or it can be pieced, for example into stars or sunshine blocks, or bordered with sawtooth edges.

 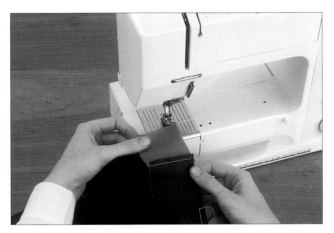

The borders and squares are cut out and stitched together before the backing is attached and the quilting completed.

GLOSSARY

ALBUM QUILT (see also AUTOGRAPH,
   MEMORY, SIGNATURE QUILT)
A quilt being made up of different blocks rather
than one or several blocks repeated throughout the
whole quilt.

AMISH QUILT
A quilt made by the Amish religious group. These
quilts are usually easily recognizable by their lack of
use of patterned fabric and their vibrant use of strong,
usually darker colors in bold large piecing patterns.

APPLIQUÉ (illustrated right)
The technique by which one piece of fabric is applied
on top of another. This technique is used when shapes
become too complicated to be pieced together.

AUTOGRAPH QUILT
  (see also SIGNATURE, ALBUM, MEMORY)
A quilt made from blocks gathered from friends and
relations and members of the community, sometimes
for an important event, such as a betrothal, wedding
etc. Blocks usually contain the signature of the donor.

BALTIMORE ALBUM QUILT
This type of quilt was very popular in the 1800s in
Baltimore, Maryland. Blocks usually consist of
complicated applique work on a white background.
The applied pieces are usually designs based on
floral or other natural subjects, predominantly in
red and green.

BINDING
The edges of a quilt are often finished off with bias or
straight-grain strips of fabric which cover the raw
edges of a quilt. This binding is often in a color that
contrasts with the background fabric of the quilt.

BLOCK
A section or piece of a quilt that makes up the whole quilt.

BORDER (illustrated above)
When a quilt is not finished off by binding, it may be completed by the use of a pattern specially designed to provide a border for the whole quilt. While the stitched pattern that holds together the quilt may extend across the whole quilt, a different pattern may be worked out to go into the corners and out to the edge of the quilt: this is the quilted, rather than the pieced border.

BRODERIE PERSE
  (also known as "cut-out chintz" or "appliquéd chintz")
This applied technique (named from the French for

"Persian embroidery") was popular in the late-nineteenth century. Birds, trees, flowers and other cut-out motifs were applied to a plain, usually white background fabric.

CALENDARED FABRIC
Fabric with a smooth finish achieved by a rotary ironing process.

CALICO
Originally the term "calico" referred to any cotton fabric that featured one or more colors other than the main color. The term refers to the Indian port, Calicut, from where these figured fabrics were first obtained. In the U.S., calico has come to mean a dress-weight cotton printed with a small pattern: in the UK it is taken to mean plain white unprinted cotton.

CALIMANCO
A worsted fabric that has been glazed or CALENDARED to give a glossy or shiny surface.

CANDLEWICKING or ROVING
Raised tufted areas on white cotton or linen. These are created by embroidering with a loosely twisted yarn that was used in the eighteenth century for making the wicks of candles. After embroidering, the created loops are clipped and when the fabric is washed, it shrinks and causes the tufts to become fluffier and appear more densely packed.

Hawaiian quilts. A single line of echo quilting is known as OUTLINE QUILTING.

FILLING OR FILLER PATTERN

Quilting that covers the entire background of a quilt. The stitching can either go right across applied or pieced pieces, following a pattern of its own or can follow the outlines of the blocks or applied pieces (see OUTLINE and ECHO QUILTING).

FRIENDSHIP QUILT

A quilt made for one person by a group of friends, each making at least one block for the quilt top and sometimes getting together to complete the quilt.

IN-THE-DITCH

Quilting stitches sewn in the "ditch" made by the seam between patchwork pieces.

LOG CABIN

A pattern in which narrow strips are built up on a foundation fabric to form a block. There are several ways to arrange the blocks to create pattern variations such as: courthouse steps, pineapple, and windmill blades.

MEDALLION QUILT

A quilt where the design is built up around one central motif or "medallion." This type of quilt usually has several borders.

CRAZY QUILT (illustrated above)

Popular in Victorian times, this type of quilting used up the tiniest scraps of fabric and was therefore quite often employed to use up scraps of expensive fabric such as velvet and satin. The joins between scraps were then covered with feather stitching or even more intricate embroidery.

ECHO QUILTING (illustrated p.125)

Lines of quilting that follow the outline of an appliquéd piece or a block. Used extensively in

MEMORY QUILT

Either a quilt made to remind a person of parts of their lives, often made from pieces of favorite garments or a quilt made in memory of deceased relative or friend.

ONE-PATCH QUILT

A quilt made from just one shape patch such as only triangles, only squares or only hexagons.

OUTLINE QUILTING

Lines of quilting running around an appliquéd piece or a block rather than across. (multiple lines are known as ECHO QUILTING)

PATCH

An individual fabric shape joined with others to make a quilt block which in turn makes up a complete quilt.

PATCHWORK (also known as PIECEWORK)

The method by which a quilt top is made up of many pieces of different fabric.

PIECED BORDER

A strip of fabric made up of pieced pieces or patches, sewn around the main part of a quilt and to provide a "frame" for the main design, just as a picture frame completes a painting. A quilt may have more than one border, just as a painting has a frame and a mount and sometimes even a double mount.

PIECING/PIECED/PATCHWORK QUILT

A quilt made up of small pieces of fabric pieced together to make a quilt top. The most simplest design is when the quilt is made of just one patchwork shape, it is then often known as a ONE PATCH QUILT.

REDWORK/BLUEWORK

Embroidered blocks done in either turkey red or blue. The embroidery was executed in very simple running stitches.

ROVING see CANDLEWICKING

SAMPLER QUILT
A quilt made up of different blocks but usually all made by the same person to try out different patterns, similar to a needlework sampler in which various stitches are gathered together to display the expertise of the maker. Sampler quilts and FRIENDSHIP and ALBUM quilts have much in common with each other in that they are made of very different blocks.

SASHING (illustrated below)
Strips of fabric between blocks that frame them and

separate them from each other. Often the sashing and the BINDING on a quilt are in the same color, thereby pulling the design together.

SIGNATURE QUILT
 (see also ALBUM and FRIENDSHIP QUILTS)
A quilt made up of blocks bearing many different signatures.

STITCH IN THE DITCH
Quilting stitches sewn in the "ditch" made by the seam between patchwork pieces.

TIED QUILT
A quilt where the layers are held together by a series of ties, rather than by quilting stitches.

TRAPUNTO (illustrated p.127)
A piece of coarse-weave fabric is basted to the back of the quilt top. The lines of the quilting design, for example vine stems and leaves, are then corded. A cord is threaded first from outside the coarse underlayer to the space between the two layers and then carefully between the two lines of fine stitches that create the line of the pattern, in this case the vine stems. The larger areas are then padded by pushing small pieces of padding through the loosely woven backing fabric until an area such as a leaf is firmly padded thus creating a design in relief.

WHITEWORK

A type of WHOLE CLOTH QUILT which is made up of white quilting stitches on an unpieced white fabric background. Sometimes areas between lines of quilting stitches are stuffed with padding. This technique is known as TRAPUNTO (from a technique developed in Italy).

WHOLE CLOTH QUILT

A quilt made of one or several large pieces of cloth, usually a solid, unpatterned color. The beauty of the quilt is derived from the elaborate quilting stitches used to hold the quilt top to the filling and the backing.

WORSTED

A woollen fabric made from well-twisted yarn spun from long-staple wool which has been combed to ensure that the fibres lay parallel to each other.

BIBLIOGRAPHY

Bishop, Robert and Safanda, Elizabeth: *Amish Quilts*; Laurence King, London, 1991.

Brackman, Barbara: *Clues in the Calico: A Guide to Identifying and Dating Antique Quilts*; EPM Publications, Inc., McLean, Virginia, 1989.

Broude, Norma and Garrard, Mary D. (ed): *The Power of Feminist Art*; Harry N. Abrahams, Inc., New York, 1994.

Colby, Avril: *Patchwork*; B.T. Batsford Ltd, London, 1958.

Fitzpatrick, Dawn: *Folk Art Applique Quilts*; Merehurst, London, 1990.

Hughes, Robert and Silber, Julie: *Amish The Art of the Quilt*; Phaidon Press Limited, London, 1974.

Kiracofe, Roderick and Johnson, Mary Elizabeth: *The American Quilt: A History of Cloth and Comfort 1750-1950*; Clarkson N. Potter, New York, 1993.

McKim, Ruby: *101 Patchwork Patterns*, 2nd ed; Dover Publications, Inc., New York, 1962.

Montgomery, Florence M.: *Printed Textiles: English and American Cottons and Linens 1700-1850*; Viking Press, New York, 1970.

Montgomery, Florence M.: *Textiles in America, 1650-1870*; W.W. Norton, New York, 1984.

Parker, Roszicka: *The Subversive Stitch: Embroidery and the Making of the Feminine*; The Women's Press Ltd, London, 1984.

Safford, Carleton L. and Bishop, Robert: *America's Quilts and Coverlets*; E.P. Dutton & Co., Inc., New York, 1972.

Wahlman, Maude Southwell: *Signs and Symbols*; Publisher, Place, Studio Books, 1993

Warren, Elizabeth V. and Eisenstat, Sharon L.: *Glorious American Quilts: The Quilt Collection of the Museum of American Folk Art*; Penguin Studio in association with the Museum of American Folk Art, 1996.